HELD
and
Beloved

Discover the passion to tell your own story of JESUS,
the One who holds you and loves you like no other!

Wendi Stewart Colaiuta

WESTBOW
PRESS®
A DIVISION OF THOMAS NELSON
& ZONDERVAN

Oh how He loves you!
~ Wendi

This book is a work of non-fiction. Unless otherwise noted, the author and the publisher make no explicit guarantees as to the accuracy of the information contained in this book and in some cases, names of people and places have been altered to protect their privacy.

WestBow Press books may be ordered through booksellers or by contacting:

WestBow Press
A Division of Thomas Nelson & Zondervan
1663 Liberty Drive
Bloomington, IN 47403
www.westbowpress.com
1 (866) 928-1240

Because of the dynamic nature of the Internet, any web addresses or links contained in this book may have changed since publication and may no longer be valid. The views expressed in this work are solely those of the author and do not necessarily reflect the views of the publisher, and the publisher hereby disclaims any responsibility for them.

Any people depicted in stock imagery provided by Getty Images are models, and such images are being used for illustrative purposes only. Certain stock imagery © Getty Images.

ISBN: 978-1-9736-7952-3 (sc)
ISBN: 978-1-9736-7953-0 (hc)
ISBN: 978-1-9736-7951-6 (e)

Library of Congress Control Number: 2019918084

Print information available on the last page.

WestBow Press rev. date: 11/13/2019

To our parents, Dad & Mom Stewart,
and Dad & Mom Colaiuta,
who first told us the story of *Jesus*,
drawing our hearts to know and trust the Savior!

Contents

Introduction

Life is hard. Sometimes heartbreakingly, bone-wearyingly hard.

Life is also precious. Sometimes breathtakingly beautiful, deeply touching, and treasured.

Seldom do we pause to really consider what holds us together when the pieces swirl, when we try to hold it all, and discover we can't. Sometimes it sneaks up on us and suddenly it all just seems too big. The joys and the struggles all wrapped up into one, mounting until they overwhelm us in a flood.

When we cry out for help, who do we truly long to come to our rescue?

Someone who knows us personally, cares for us deeply, and is fully capable of changing our reality from impossible to manageable. When that transformation also brings blessings in disguise, we are humbled by extravagant grace.

How might our hearts shift to know that there *is* Someone who can meet all those longings? And not just any someone, but the One and only Someone who is eternally unchanging and unfailingly trustworthy! The only Someone who knows us better than any other and loves us more than anyone ever could. The only Someone who is strong enough and sovereign enough and kind enough and wise enough—to hold all the pieces, to hold us together, no matter what!

His Name is JESUS. He is my most precious Someone. And I am precious to Him!

Over the past year, through some of the greatest joys and trials I have ever experienced, #trustingJESUS has become an emboldening reminder to me! Daily. Sometimes hourly. My sweet sisters surprised me with a bracelet for my fiftieth birthday with that hashtag inscribed on its face. I wear it so often I fear the engraving will fade or the metal will grow too thin to hold together.

But the truth will remain. His Name is JESUS. He is my Savior. And I can trust Him. Always.

How has He become so precious to me? How do I know how precious I am to Him?

What has won my heart to place my trust in the LORD JESUS? Who is He and what gives me the confidence to claim His hand upon my life as its single steadying force?

Held and Beloved tells that story. It doesn't make headlines. But it is mine. And I want to be faithful to tell it! I want to bear witness of the reality of GOD in my life. My struggles run the gamut from bewilderingly perplexing to deeply painful. They are the tender places where I encounter JESUS. They tell the story of the battle ground where He wins my heart.

I could not possibly tell my story without including the testimonies of women, just like me, whose lives date back to the beginning of time. Seeing how women in the Bible encountered GOD and how He marvelously worked through their circumstances to meet their needs and win their hearts has brought comfort, clarity, and peace to me! These treasured women surround me. Together, we tell of His heart as we share our stories.

True for you too? What story has He given you to tell, in your own way? To bear witness of the reality of GOD in your life?

May our stories help you find your own voice. To speak truth as you have experienced it—large and undeniable and life-changing! This is the only kind of impact our GOD and Savior makes on a life!

In my book, it *is* newsworthy. Good News, gospel-worthy!

ℴℹ . ℴℹ

When I was deciding which stories of women in the Bible I wanted to share along with my own, I discovered a wondrous string of pairings! Each chapter tells the story of a woman from the old testament and one from the new (or multiple from each), who walked through circumstances unique to each of them, but who encountered a similar aspect of the heart of GOD.

Sarah and Elizabeth both experienced GOD doing the impossible within their physical bodies. Hagar and Mary Magdalene both heard the LORD speak their names. Women who reached out to GOD's prophet Elisha and women who desperately needed JESUS' healing touch all came to know the LORD as the One who is never limited and never too late! And more . . .

I thought I knew these stories well. But taking a closer look at them led to fresh and amazing discoveries! I am deeply grateful to a small circle of friends who gathered weekly in my living room this summer to share insights from these passages. If these stories are not familiar to you, at the end of each chapter, please look for the Bible references we used to read their full accounts and questions that helped us delve into the experiences of these women and reflect on our own.

Lingering over these details, imagining what it might have been like to stand in these women's shoes, helped me to better understand my own times of struggle, questions, doubts and pain. Joining the conversation with them, giving honor to the One who meets us in every one of those moments, brought clarity and healing I didn't expect. At times, I was simply overwhelmed to realize the hand of GOD upon my life. The threads of His purposes woven through decades, but also through the trials of recent years that sometimes still feel fresh and raw, have been leading me to know Him, the exactness of His plan, and the immeasurable depth of His love!

ℬ . ℭ

What a joy it will be to journey through these pages, rejoicing in the One who is the same yesterday, today, and forever! What was true of Almighty GOD to each of these women has been true for me—and is true for you too! Dear reader, will you come along with us and join the conversation?

I pray that as you see His hand working and moving in our stories, you will begin to recognize His presence and His touch on your own. That you will know that you, too, are *Held and Beloved* by the One who gave everything to be your Savior! That you will find your own voice to tell the story He has uniquely and wondrously given you to tell!

Chapter One

the *One* with whom nothing is impossible: blessed is she who believes

Another hour passed as the clock ticked in the dark of night. She struggled to sleep but couldn't. In those days, mamas didn't stay in the hospital room overnight with their little ones. They walked out with everyone else at the end of visiting hours.

Despite willing herself *not* to go, this young mama had done just that, leaving her three-month-old baby girl in a padded crib at St. Christopher's Children's Hospital in Philadelphia. She went home to spend some time with her husband and two-year-old daughter. To try to rest. And pray. And wait.

In the darkness, she found herself pleading for morning to come and yet dreading it all at the same time. There was no news through the night and she never knew what morning would reveal. She wanted to believe each new day would be the day that healing would come. She feared each new day could be the day they lost her. And the truth is, she never knew how close they came on more than one occasion.

Agonizing weeks passed as a blood vessel tumor held her baby girl's right forearm captive. It was blown up like an oversized eggplant, equally purple in color. It was sucking every last platelet out of her little body, leaving her vulnerable to bleeding that couldn't be stopped, which would be fatal.

There were only five cases of this type of hemangioma on record. Their pediatrician stayed up many nights making calls, hunting down any available information that would help. In the days before cell phones or even beepers, this doctor had given his home telephone number. He insisted they call day or night if they needed anything, even if it was just a reassuring voice that someone cared enough to work around the clock to save their baby girl.

Many family members and friends were praying. It gave them hope and confidence that couldn't be explained. A peace that no matter the news of the day, a loving heavenly Father was over all things. He would be with their baby girl when they couldn't. He who formed her body was able to heal it.

At a critical time when all seemed hopeless, a daunting rescue plan was seriously discussed. Amputation. It seemed the only way to remove the tumor and allow the body to return to normal. But without an arm. How could they make such a life-altering decision for their three-month-old baby girl?

Impossible. It all seemed insurmountable. How could they begin to understand which path forward was best? To properly sift through medical updates they could barely make sense of? Their baby's condition was so rare, even the professionals seemed at a loss for a confident recommendation.

Prayers continued for wisdom beyond their comprehension.

Practical concerns began to haunt them. Could they even imagine what life would be like for their little girl without an arm? Would they know how to help her navigate the adjustments she would need to make? Could such a daring plan truly be the lifesaving measure they longed for? How could they make this terrifying decision?

It all seemed impossible.

ॐ . ೞ

Many, many years before, another woman faced her own "impossibles." Insurmountable circumstances. Terrifying decisions. Feelings of inadequacy, fear, uncertainty.

Sarah's husband, Abraham, was known as "the friend of GOD,"[1] the One who called them to leave their home and travel to an unknown land. With little explanation to offer anyone who asked, they obeyed. They packed up their belongings, household, and flocks, and started their journey.

They spent many years following without really knowing how GOD would fulfill His plans, but holding dearly to His promises— of land, of innumerable descendants, of His protection and the great reward of His Presence, of a covenant with Almighty GOD, and that Abraham would become the father of a great nation through whom all nations of the world would be blessed.

Sarah was Abraham's "princess."[2] She was beautiful and treasured. But she was barren. Unable to conceive and bear the children the LORD promised. How did she fit into the plans GOD revealed to her husband? Was she part of His plan? Did she matter to Him? Being barren was already viewed as a disgrace in her culture. To make matters worse, she couldn't begin to understand how her reality fit into GOD's purposes. Heaviness often clouded her heart. Leaving her feeling more cursed than blessed.

Very likely, there were times of raging doubt and confusion, trying to make sense of GOD's plans when they seemed so contrary to human reasoning. How did Sarah feel about GOD's call on her husband's life or their new, transient existence? Did she find it adventurous and exciting? A chance to escape the judgmental glances or hard questions from others that she never could answer? Or did it leave her weary, lonely, questioning, and longing—still longing for a child and now also longing for anything that felt like "home?" What did she think of the GOD to whom her husband seemed so loyal, so convinced of His existence and sovereignty?

Scripture doesn't say. But we know that when GOD called

Abraham, they found enough courage to obey and followed the path to which GOD pointed.

There were faltering steps along the way, when fear and impatience led to unwise and ungodly decisions. When Abraham asked her to protect him by saying he was her brother so heathen political leaders would not kill him in order to claim his wife for themselves. Sarah was taken into those rulers' harems, alone and in danger in foreign lands, with only the unseen hand of GOD moving behind the scenes to protect and rescue her. Or when the fulfillment of GOD's promise of a son was too long in coming, Sarah was the one who offered the alternative path of using a surrogate mother. But that choice only complicated their struggles with deeper strife, heartache, separation, and blame.

It all seemed horribly impossible.

In the middle of their mess, Abraham still seemed confident. But Sarah was not. Her insides swirled with a growing mixture of frustration, deepening confusion, and painful disappointment. She resigned herself to never understanding this GOD Abraham trusted so unwaveringly.

But GOD!

One memorable day, three men came to visit Abraham and Sarah in the desert. Abraham quickly directed his men to prepare meat and Sarah to bake cakes for their visitors. As her husband dined with the men in the shade outside, Sarah hid in the tent, straining to hear their conversation. She heard Abraham speak to one of the men the way he had often spoken to the LORD! Could he be meeting with this GOD face to face? What would the LORD say to him during this miraculous visit?

Did Sarah hear Him correctly? The LORD reiterated His plans for Abraham to have a son. Only this time, He spoke Sarah's name! He made it clear that His covenant promises would not be fulfilled through a surrogate mother's child, but through Sarah's son! He confidently stated that Sarah would bear a son and name him Isaac.

Sarah couldn't contain her shock and disbelief and laughed out loud! How on earth could that be possible? She was nearly ninety years old and Abraham nearly one hundred! She had never been able to conceive a child and her body was now long past child-bearing age! It all seemed too ridiculous to consider.

The LORD spoke again, asking why Sarah had laughed. She had been discovered! He saw her. He heard her. Embarrassed and possibly for the first time, feeling fear of Almighty GOD, Sarah denied that she laughed. But the LORD knew her heart. He stated the facts, "That is not true. You did laugh."[3]

She held her breath. How would the LORD respond to her disbelief? Her dishonesty?

But how gracious is He? His plans were not deterred by her faltering steps. He spoke plainly to Abraham in her hearing, "Is anything too hard for the LORD? About a year from now, just as I told you, I will return, and Sarah will have a son."[4]

Beyond human comprehension and the laws of physical science (as only GOD can do!), Sarah and Abraham would have a child! Sarah may not have spoken to the LORD face to face as Abraham had, but she heard His voice. She heard Him identify her by name and promise the impossible. She would come to know in the very depths of her being that *nothing* is too hard for the LORD!

I wonder if that day behind the tent door was a turning point for Sarah? She heard the One true GOD speak her name and proclaim with assurance that His promise would be fulfilled through her! Was that the moment when she realized the certainty of His promise was not up to her or to Abraham? Not dependent on the state of their physical bodies or even remotely jeopardized by her disbelief? It was simply GOD's doing—and *nothing* is impossible with Him!

*"...e Lord who created you says:
Do not be afraid, for I have
ransomed you. I have called you by
name; you are Mine."*

Isaiah 43:1

Hebrews tells us that Sarah believed GOD would keep His promise, that she judged Him faithful. Reading her story, I am not so sure that was always the case. We aren't told much about Sarah's journey of faith in GOD. But it seems that now she was not just taking Abraham's word for it, not just following his lead as head of their home. This was her personal moment of trusting GOD! And maybe for the first time, she stood confidently with her husband, knowing that Almighty GOD saw them as one and that together they would see Him accomplish great things!

It is wonderful to consider that the LORD pursued her heart, personally and intimately, until she was able to trust Him.

I find it heartwarming that the LORD named their son Isaac, which means "laughter." Sarah would finally be a mom! She would feel him growing inside her. She would know the elation of hearing his first cry after the pain of labor. She would rock and bounce a baby in her arms and sing him to sleep. She would watch him grow and note each milestone.

Sarah would know a deeper joy than she could imagine. True laughter, not of disbelief, but of awe and worship with which nothing could compare. Soul-strengthening joy that could only come from GOD taking their "impossibles" and showing them exactly what He can do—immeasurably, abundantly, and above all that they could imagine! His plans were always exact and right on time. Moving forward in a way that was undeniably, exclusively *His* doing!

Sarah was able to have a child,
though she was barren and was too old.
She believed that God would keep
His promise.

Hebrews 11:11

℘ . ℭ

Hundreds of years after Sarah, another precious woman wrestled similar "impossibles."

Born into the priestly line of Aaron, Elizabeth and her husband Zechariah clung to the same promises given to their ancestor, Abraham. They served the LORD faithfully, trusting in His continued protection and the great reward of His presence. They watched expectantly for the fulfillment of His greatest promise: from their nation the promised Messiah would come.

Some days it was harder than others to hold that hope! Centuries had gone by. It became more difficult with each passing year to find glimpses that Almighty GOD was still at work, His plan in perfect step despite any visible evidence.

Elizabeth also carried a private ache, a similarly cultural disgrace that echoed Sarah's. She was barren.

By the time we are introduced to Elizabeth, both she and her husband are well advanced in years, far beyond child-bearing age. She had spent decades waiting for a child, longing to raise a son who could learn from his father to serve GOD in His temple.

In a family of priests, their role within the nation of Israel was already set apart. Zechariah and Elizabeth were both descendants of Levi, the only extended family line of their patriarch Jacob, also known as Israel, that was called by GOD to serve Him as their sole occupation. They represented GOD to the people, teaching them

His law and His ways, and offered sacrifices from the people to the LORD. GOD called Elizabeth to walk a path that was additionally isolating, misunderstood, and probably lonely—as a childless woman in the tribe of Levi, where she might have felt her singular purpose was to birth and raise a new generation of priests.

The waiting. More than any specific challenge, the long days, weeks, and years of waiting and wondering, praying and watching, and surrendering the haunting questions again and again, those were likely the most painful. Any hope she once held of raising a son for the LORD's purposes was long ago relinquished. What place did she hold in GOD's plans? She simply gave her best to whatever task was in front of her, to serve GOD in any way available to her. But some days, the disappointment might have seemed impossibly hard to overcome.

Then, when they least expected it, Elizabeth and Zechariah were given the remarkable opportunity to see how their unique situation would draw attention to the truly miraculous things GOD was about to do.

An angel from GOD appeared to Zechariah, telling him their prayers had been heard and answered. Elizabeth, who was called barren and beyond child-bearing age, would conceive, carry, birth, and raise a son! Their child was named and claimed by GOD, for a specific and thrilling assignment before he was even conceived.

Unimaginable. Beyond human comprehension and physical science. Yet in her very body, Elizabeth experienced the impossible become possible!

After a lifetime of faithful service to GOD, she and her extended family were chosen to live out critical details of the LORD's eternal plan of redemption for His people. After generations of longing, they were watching it all unfold. In their very own home, but also with a far-reaching impact they couldn't begin to understand.

Elizabeth's recorded words are few but very telling: "How kind the LORD is! He has taken away my disgrace."[5]

When Elizabeth was six months pregnant, a much younger woman, her cousin Mary, was chosen by GOD to carry and birth His Son, the promised Messiah. Remarkably, Elizabeth held no envy or questions. She genuinely rejoiced with Mary, proclaiming her blessed and marveling at the thought that the mother of her LORD would come to visit her!

> *You are blessed, because you believed that the Lord would do what He said.*

Luke 1:45

Elizabeth warmly welcomed Mary into her home for the first three months of her own pregnancy. Two women, generations apart in age, yet uniquely called by GOD to walk equally unusual and probably misunderstood paths to motherhood, were given the gift of supporting one another in the quiet, tucked-away place of Elizabeth's home.

How did Elizabeth stay so calm, so confident, so joyfully yielded? How did she seem to know and understand what GOD was doing? I can only guess that her unique circumstances (those personal struggles that left her so lonely at times) led her to the LORD in prayer many times over many years. She had listened and learned His commands and promises and believed them. The one true GOD made Himself real to her in a growing, personal way. He held her aching heart and revealed things to her that few people knew or understood.

He was not just the GOD who offered promises that could be trusted, but a GOD who heard and knew and understood. The One who saw beyond the disgrace that seemed to overwhelm her, the One who had a unique and treasured place for her in His much bigger plan.

Knowing God and trusting His plan must have steadied her when she found herself in uncharted territory. When no one knew quite what to make of their living miracle, she seemed to have no questions, only confidence. And joy! Her life before, during and after giving birth to her long-awaited son seems to have been hidden away, quiet, unnoticed by most, simply faithful.

God noticed. God placed her exactly where she was, mapped out her days, and had eternal purposes embedded in each step. He asked her to walk a difficult and heart-breaking path but equipped her to do so. He commended her faithfulness, her careful choice to follow what He revealed to her. And He used her to raise the man who would go before Him to point many in Israel to their true Messiah.

Elizabeth lived what others could then witness and understand. The coming Messiah was not just a Redeemer, but the One with whom nothing is impossible!

ဆ . ಣ

Fifty years ago, I was that baby girl fighting for life against impossible odds. My mom and dad endured long days and nights waiting and praying and never quite knowing what a new day would bring.

When the walls started to close in, they looked up. It was the same LORD who steadied them through uncharted territory!

They cried out to the only One they knew would be wise enough and sovereign enough and loving enough to direct them to the perfect solution. He held their aching hearts and gave them courage to believe He was trustworthy.

Suddenly, the tumor began to die on its own. They would not need to make the impossible decisions that weighed so heavily on their hearts. There was no real explanation. Beyond human comprehension and physical science. They simply considered it the gracious hand of God. Their personal living miracle!

It would take nearly two years for my arm to return to normal. I learned to tuck my little "eggplant" under my belly when I started to crawl, or hold it up over my head, somehow finding just the right position to offer balance as I learned to walk. I was alive! And healing. And thriving! It was hard for my mom to fight back tears as they sang to me on my first birthday and watched me blow out my candles with joy and glee that seemed oblivious to the fight I had endured.

GOD was faithful. He heard and answered all those prayers. He granted a miracle and spared my life. The promises in Psalm 139 took on new meaning. Every day of my life was written in the His book before one of them came to be. It is staggering to think that He has a unique place for me in His eternal plans. With His full purposes for my life yet to be realized, my days on earth were protected by His sovereign hand.

During those anxious days, my parents sensed the LORD's presence in fresh and tender ways. With each new, unthinkable bend in the road, He faithfully revealed Himself as the One with whom nothing is impossible!

ℴ . ℻

Read more of their stories . . . and reflect on your own!

SARAH
Genesis 12:1–9, 16:1–6, 17:15–19, 18:9–15, 21:1–7

What in Sarah's story would have challenged you the most?

What might have given her courage to meet those challenges?

In what ways did the LORD make Himself known to her?

What do you think the LORD most wanted Sarah to know about Him?

ELIZABETH
Luke 1–2

What was unique about the path the LORD asked Elizabeth to walk?

How did she describe/approach the joys and challenges in her life?

Which verses give us a glimpse of what the LORD saw in Elizabeth's heart?

What did Elizabeth recognize as the LORD's kindness to her?

How did the LORD honor Elizabeth?

OVERALL

What do you learn about GOD from their stories?

How might those aspects of His character help you navigate your own "impossibles?"

What promises has GOD given to you personally?

In what ways has He stretched the known physical/medical limits to do the "impossible" in your life? to make Himself real to you?

What is your place in His plan? (if you're not sure, He would love for you to ask Him!)

How does the LORD let you know you are treasured? valued? important? included?

℘ . ℭ

Who is this One we are getting to know more intimately?

The LORD revealed Himself to Sarah and Elizabeth as:

* the One who hears
* the One who answers in ways we don't expect, defying what we see as impossible
* the One whose promises include us
* the One who is faithful
* the One who views us as important—to Him, to our marriages, to His grand plan
* the One who rescues us from sadness, disgrace and despair
* the One who brings laughter
* the One whose timetable is orchestrated from a place of love

Chapter Two

the One who comes to my defense: blessed is she who is not condemned

An unidentified woman was caught in the very act of adultery. Dragged out into the courtyard, in front of the crowd, to be accused and probably stoned. That was the law. She was alone. Defenseless. Her mind was racing, wondering how this whole scene could have been different.

Why was she, alone, thrust into this glowing spotlight? A pawn in the religious leaders' self-righteous pursuit of their own interpretation of GOD's laws? Did anyone really care to hear her story? The circumstances surrounding her, the choices that may or may not have been her own, leading her into the downward spiral to condemnation. Was there anything, anyone who could save her now?

She couldn't even look up. She just stared at her feet. The men's voices were harsh and angry. She braced herself for the hurling stones.

Instead, there were new questions from the men. Questions directed at Someone else. She wasn't sure they were any more interested in His answers than hers, but she was thankful for the interruption. Could she even dare to hope that this could end some other way?

Before carrying out their heated judgment, the men seemed to want to know what this other Man, JESUS, thought they should do. He didn't answer them right away and stooped to write something in the dirt. Their questions persisted, so He simply said, "let those who have never sinned throw the first stones."[6]

There was suddenly an awkward silence and not-so-subtle shifting of feet. And then, miraculously, one by one, the angry, determined men dropped their stones and walked away.

She was left alone with JESUS. He spoke softly to her and asked her, "Where are your accusers? Didn't even one of them condemn you?" Somehow, she found her voice and answered Him, "No, LORD."[7] She couldn't believe this unexpected turn of events and began to wonder if she was dreaming! Then she heard the unthinkable.

Jesus said, "Neither do I condemn you. Go and sin no more."

John 8:11

I believe it was a moment of more than just words. I believe their eyes met. Maybe not before He said those words, but possibly after she heard His heart, she had the courage to look into His eyes and *know* He was her Savior.

She might not have known much about Him, but He had shown the power and authority to proclaim her free of condemnation. She might not have realized it yet, but *He* would pay the penalty for her sin and set her free.

Do I believe she felt those words gave her license? That it was okay, that He understood why her life was the way it was, that

He didn't condemn her, so it must be all right? Not for a second! He clearly said to her, "Go, and sin no more."[8]

Do I believe her encounter with Jesus was a game-changer in her life, the turning point after which she no longer wrestled with that sin? It is entirely possible!

Overwhelming victory is ours through Christ, who loves us.

Romans 8:37

Do I believe it is also possible that the "sin that so easily hinders our progress"[9] reared its ugly head again in her life? Sadly, this is also possible. Even as His redeemed children, we still wrestle against our sinful flesh, in ourselves or in others.

Do I believe if He encountered her again, entangled in the same sin, that He would say the same words to her? Without a doubt, Yes! I believe He would have pursued a meeting with her again, and again, and again, if necessary, to tell her that His payment for her sin never expires!

This is grace! Our Savior's mercies that are new every morning! But, do we willfully choose to sin again, and again, and again, because His grace covers us? As Paul says in Romans, "God forbid"[10] that we should handle the mercy of God so recklessly! Would taking His grace for granted not sorely grieve the Savior's heart? Would such a willful choice to remain in a sinful path not deeply dishonor the lengths He went to secure redemption for us? The sacrifice He suffered to offer us a payment that never expires?

May we receive with grateful hearts the freedom He offers us from the penalty of sin. But may our gratefulness not stop short of worship and honor of the One who died so we can walk in that freedom—from the penalty of sin, but also from the power of sin! May we not stop short of utterly transformed desires that are committed to choices that delight rather than grieve His heart. May we reach for His help to win the battle against our sin-bent flesh again, and again, and again.

℘ . ℭ

A woman named Gomer was trapped in a cycle that continued to spiral out of control. Blinded by the lie that chasing other loves would satisfy her more. More than the faithful love and abundant provisions of her husband, Hosea.

Clarity would strike on the darkest days. Alone and battered, facing the harsh truth that she had been deceived. She'd been running after a dissipating illusion of flashy attention and affection, instead of gratefully receiving the beautiful reality and security her husband freely offered her.

Her choices had broken Hosea's heart, caused him so much pain, separation, and loss. She had cut herself off from him. How could she ever look him in the face?

Tangled, lonely, and increasingly desperate, sometimes Gomer still thought about returning. But she could never take the first step to turn around. She was incapable of the rescue she truly needed.

To her surprise, her husband came looking for her! The LORD spoke to Hosea's heart and directed him to pursue Gomer, to bring her home again. Acknowledging the pain, the shame he would take on himself, the possibility of future, repeated betrayal, the LORD called Hosea to love like He does. To count the cost and love anyway!

It may have been a kind of love even Hosea struggled to grasp. Unconditional. Self-sacrificing. At any cost. No matter what. Faithful and enduring.

It seems even more likely that genuine, authentic love was completely foreign to Gomer. Did she recognize it? Did she understand it? Was it easier to return again and again to the "known and comfortable," the passing fancies of glitz and attention from other suitors? Was she so deeply wounded that she didn't feel worthy of true love?

This is the beautiful thing about GOD's love. It *is* the real thing! It is love with capacity to grow rather than wear us out or disappoint us. His love pursues us. His love takes the blows on Himself so He can freely offer us the security of true devotion and provision. His love never fails. His love always wins!

The LORD called Hosea to do the hard thing. To risk everything to love anyway. Although he was not responsible for Gomer's betrayal, he paid the price to set her free, to restore her to his love and care. His actions reached beyond the inclination of his human heart. He was no longer just her husband. Now he was also her redeemer. He stepped in to do for her what she was incapable of doing for herself.

(And maybe in that moment, Hosea understood, as well, the depth of his own Redeemer's sacrificial love for him!)

Gomer could finally breathe again. She could stop chasing what always left her empty. She could stop fighting a losing battle. She could simply say "Thank you," let Hosea take her hand in his and lead her home.

Up to that point, Gomer had only seen Hosea as "lord," customarily recognizing him as master of their home. At last, she saw him with different eyes, calling him her "husband," her partner in GOD's covenant of marriage. He was not just the one who was responsible for her, but the one who loved her enough to pursue her, to give everything to secure her place right by his side. To bring her home.

The LORD used Hosea and Gomer's marriage to demonstrate His redemptive love for Israel:

I will win her back once again.
I will lead her out into the desert and
speak tenderly to her there. I will return

her vineyards to her and transform the Valley of Trouble into a gateway of hope. . . I will be faithful to you and make you mine, and you will finally know Me as Lord.

Hosea 2:14–15, 20

೮ . ೦ଓ

Guilty. A sinner before holy, Almighty GOD. With no excuse and no defense.

I knew it. It made my heart race and my stomach churn.

I remember that Monday. It was the first day of summer vacation from elementary school. I lingered in bed, deep in thought about a question posed in a gospel message at church the night before: "are you SURE of heaven?"

My honest answer was, "No."

No, I wasn't sure, and I wasn't sure how to become sure. I believed the Bible to be GOD's Word. I didn't doubt the reality of Almighty Creator GOD or that His words were true. So why wasn't I confident that I would be with Him in heaven one day?

Because sin separates. Unanswered, it makes us uncomfortable in front of the One to whom we must give an account.

I wrestled with all I knew about JESUS, GOD's Son, suffering on the cross to be my Savior, to pay the penalty for my sin, the one thing keeping me from peace with GOD. But I kept thinking I was missing something. What was I supposed to do? To think? To believe? How exactly was I to find the confidence in my eternal security I longed to know?

Even at age 12, I was over-thinking everything, desperately searching for anything *I could do* to ensure my own salvation. But there was nothing.

Then, I heard the LORD's still, small voice for the very first time. He broke through all my confusion and brought one simple verse to my mind and heart:

Jesus said, "It is finished."

John 19:30

My mental gymnastics melted away in that moment. JESUS had *finished* the work of securing my salvation. He did what I was incapable of doing for myself. He had already paid the price to set me free from condemnation!

My salvation wasn't dependent upon me at all. The only sinless Man to ever walk this earth met the requirements of righteous GOD—for me! What more did I need?

A brief moment of doubt crept back in. Could it be that simple?

Yes! It absolutely is that simple.

GOD said it, I believe it, that finishes it.

Decades later I am more profoundly thankful than ever for my Savior's complete work of redemption on my behalf. I take GOD at His Word, for He is trustworthy. Because He says that JESUS died for me, that I can be forgiven and righteous in GOD's sight, and live with Him in the glory one day, I can now say *I am sure of heaven!*

I no longer squirm uncomfortably before Him. Because of JESUS, Almighty GOD does not condemn me. I am welcomed into His embrace as His redeemed child. He speaks words of tender comfort and reassurance to my heart. Nothing will ever snatch me from His hand!

&. ଔ

This is our Savior, who pursues us. Again and again and again. To remind us:

There is no condemnation for those who belong to Christ Jesus!

Romans 8:1

The consequences of sin are harsh. There is no sugar-coating it. Sin is rebellion against GOD and leads only to destruction and death. Holy GOD longs for us to know the seriousness of GODless choices. He pursues our hearts to lead us to true repentance, a deeply personal decision to choose Him, His salvation, His ways, and His plan. He knows when we turn to Him, we are open and ready to receive His best for us. Full restoration and everlasting, vibrant life.

The life He gives is eternal, the payment He made for our sin is once-for-all. Not for some of our sin, not for most of our sin, but for *all* of our sin. That's why He died. His sacrifice is the only one that can cover us—always and forever, amen!

I assure you, those who listen to My message, and believe in God who sent Me, have eternal life.
They will never be condemned for their sins, but they have already passed from death into life.

John 5:24

ॐ . ॐ

Read more of their stories . . . and reflect on your own!

THE ADULTEROUS WOMAN
John 8:1–11

Why/how was this woman found guilty?

What options were available to her in navigating her complicated story?

What might have been her thoughts or fears?

What did JESUS reveal about Himself to her?

In what complicated moments has JESUS come to your side to offer redemption?

GOMER
Hosea 1–3

What was unique about Gomer's marriage to Hosea?

What temptations tugged at Gomer's heart?

What different story did Hosea offer her?

How did the LORD work in Hosea's heart to pursue her?

How did the LORD use their marriage to demonstrate His love for Israel?

OVERALL
Romans 8, Psalm 32

What sin in your life makes it uncomfortable for you to seek GOD's face?

What Bible verses tell you what JESUS has done to pay the penalty for your sin and set you free?

How does your heart respond, knowing that because of JESUS, Almighty GOD says you are not condemned?

ℂ . ℃

Who is this One we are getting to know more intimately?

The LORD revealed Himself to the adulterous woman and Gomer as:

* the One who pursues our hearts, bringing us to repentance
* the One who loves us unconditionally, no matter what
* the One who has the power to redeem and restore us
* the One who pays the penalty and sets us free
* the One who removes our shame
* the One who draw us to His side

Chapter Three

the One who gives me a new story: blessed is she who aligns with the one true God

A courageous woman named Rahab lived in a home built into the walls of the city of Jericho. She had heard about GOD's people. A new nation. A miraculous rescue from the mighty land of Egypt. Awe-inspiring stories about guidance from cloud and from fire, water from a rock, and daily provision of food from the heavens. Something about their journey captured her heart. She longed to know more.

It was interesting enough to watch from afar as they wandered the desert. But news was rolling in, rising panic around her. Their path seemed more determined. Their end goal a land that was promised to them as a permanent possession. Her land. Her city!

She couldn't imagine the details that would be orchestrated to bring those promises to fulfillment. But she was beginning to understand that these were not random whims of a crazed group of wandering, homeless travelers. There was exactness to their movements, power behind their victories.

Others in her town shook in fear. This mysterious power and unknown campaign terrified them. But she saw it all differently.

The years and the stories all pointed in one direction. Bearing witness of the One who had chosen His people, led them and blessed them, and called them to help others come to know Him. Almighty Creator GOD. The one and only true and living GOD. Maker of heaven and earth!

He was not an image, a breathless piece of wood or stone. No. He was real. He was powerful. His ways were wondrous. And she wanted to know Him!

Scriptures tell us plainly that Rahab was a prostitute living in Jericho. She was not one of GOD's chosen people. She may have thought that her story was one that would disqualify her from ever being chosen.

None of that stopped her. When given the chance, she risked everything to align herself with the one true GOD, to protect the men who were serving His purposes, and to boldly ask for His protection in return.

When two spies from Israel's camp entered Jericho on a reconnaissance mission, Rahab welcomed them into her home. She risked her own life to protect them, hiding them on her rooftop when messengers from the king came to find them. In return, she presented her daring request:

"I know that the LORD has given you this land . . . that the LORD your GOD is GOD in heaven and earth. Please swear to me by the LORD that you will also show kindness to my family, because I showed kindness to you. Give me a sure sign that you will spare the lives of my father, mother, brothers, sisters, and all who belong to them, and save us from death."[11]

The men gave Rahab their promise of protection. They instructed her to hang a scarlet cord from her window on the city wall. And to bring all her family members under her roof.

The LORD honored her reach for rescue, her courageous faith in Him. When GOD brought down the walls of Jericho, Joshua directed his men to keep their word to Rahab. They broke through the chaos, found the home with the scarlet cord, and brought Rahab and her family out of the rubble, unharmed. Rahab's family settled in a safe place near this new nation of Israel.

In time, the LORD drew her even closer. She married into GOD's chosen nation and bore a son who would be a distant forefather of the promised Messiah.

The reality of GOD touched Rahab's heart. Rather than shrink in fear of His power, she placed her faith in it to save her. Could it have been mysterious kindness that allowed terrifying circumstances to surround her? That brought her to a place so desperate that she understood her deep need of the GOD who is trustworthy? That gave her boldness to take a stand few around her chose to take? Would she have risked so much to reach for the LORD's rescue if the walls were not collapsing around her?

She had the courage to believe the one true GOD would hear and respond to her cries. She had the faith to believe her story wasn't over—it was only beginning.

> *By faith Rahab the prostitute gave a friendly welcome to the spies and did not die with the others because she obeyed God.*

Hebrews 11:31

ౠ . ౧

It wasn't the way I would have written my story. I never planned on this turn of events. Not for one minute.

Some serious challenges in my young marriage were completely out of my control. They unfolded around me and I was powerless to change their course.

The red flags of caution I should have heeded before the wedding haunted me. I stubbornly chose to push past them. A young twenty-something and overconfident, I foolishly assumed *I* could make the difference. I was sure *I* could positively impact the outcome if I simply cared enough, persevered enough, stayed faithful and present and determined.

But I was wrong. My marriage failed. And I was left holding the pieces of so many broken promises and broken dreams. My tidy little picture of "happily ever after" was a myth that vanished like the mist.

I felt betrayed, deceived into living a lie. Drawn into a relationship, the covenant of marriage, built on beliefs and assumptions about my partner that were untrue. It crushed me to realize I had pledged my vows to a person that didn't exist. A persona that was fabricated to achieve goals I knew nothing about. To hide from harsh pieces of his past he hadn't fully recovered from. Until it all caught up with him, and he realized he wasn't capable of keeping up the charade.

Rather than work through those challenges to build a new foundation with GOD's help, he chose another path. And I was left alone to make sense of what seemed cruelly senseless to me.

I longed for something *real*. Something true and trustworthy I could grasp, knowing it was unsinkable. I wanted cold, hard facts, regardless of how severe. At least I could trust their validity.

The harsh realization is that I had been busy test driving my own plans while the LORD was hovering close, patiently waiting for me to choose His best. He allowed my faulty assumptions to fail, my ill-placed faith in the "pretty little picture," even though it was brutally painful, so I could understand how much I needed Him. In that place, He knew I would desperately cry out for His help and reach for His wisdom that is unshakable.

In the tailspin of those painful days, I knew it was the LORD who held me together. Private moments when tears turned to sobs, when my whole being ached for comfort, I sensed His arms around me. His Words brought healing and hope. *He* was the One who was sure and steadfast, unchangeably reliable. I could trust Him!

Let all that I am wait quietly before God, for my hope is in Him. He alone is my rock and my salvation, my fortress where I will not be shaken.

Psalm 62:5–6

One great fear broke my heart more than any other. Had I ruined everything? Did my foolishness permanently mar my life for GOD? Could He no longer use me for His purposes because my story now disqualified me from ever being chosen?

Divorced. I couldn't shake the shame. Because of CHRIST, my missteps were forgiven, but was I expected to live out my days under the radar, quietly in a corner somewhere, just waiting for the glory of heaven to make all things new again?

No. Praise GOD, His answer to my burdened heart was "No."

One precious morning, I opened my eyes to see the sun streaming through the window on a crisp, clear day. His Spirit brought the dawn of new realization to my heart. That's when I knew.

If the LORD had no other purpose for me on this earth, He would call me home to heaven right then and there. But He didn't. He awakened me to the beauty of a new day! To His new mercies, fresh every morning!

My Savior is not deterred by what's broken in my story. He died to redeem me and remove my shame. He tenderly lifts my chin and reminds me He has more than enough power and love to write the story from here. When I align my heart with His and surrender the pen, I can be sure there is more to this story—and the very best parts are yet to come!

I have loved you with an everlasting love, with loving kindness I have drawn you. I will build you up again.

Jeremiah 31:3-4

ဆ . ၄

An unidentified woman from the village of Samaria took a deep breath and headed out the door. The sun beat hot and dry on her walk to the outskirts of town, but the cooler part of the day risked meeting too many people with too many questions she didn't want to answer. Questions about her complicated relationships swirled enough in her own head and she was weary of trying to come up with explanations. The water pot on her shoulder felt heavier than usual, even before there was any water in it. The haunting details of her life seemed to sink her as deep as the well from which she would draw the water. Hurtful choices and decisions made by herself and others had left her deeply wounded. Broken.

In her brokenness, and in that place she specifically went to avoid meeting face to face with anyone, she met the one Someone she desperately needed to know. JESUS had purposely detoured to her side of town—to have a personal encounter with her!

Without hesitation, JESUS broke through her assumptions that He, being a man and of Jewish descent, would not interact with her. To her surprise, He comfortably struck up conversation. Unlike the townspeople she worked hard to avoid, He had different questions for her. He simply asked her for a drink of water, helping her to feel equally comfortable conversing with Him.

When she was willing to engage in dialogue with Him, He revealed that He had something to offer her—a well of living water springing up to eternal life, inside of her!

Once Jesus had her attention by offering her living water (which she was immediately eager to receive, but failed to fully understand), He cut right to the chase: "go call your husband."[12] He wasn't interested in a juicy tale of gossip. He wanted to reach her heart, the private struggles never breathed to anyone else.

She answered honestly. She had no husband. Then Jesus spoke the personal ache she couldn't imagine Him knowing, let alone understanding. She had had five husbands and the man she was currently living with was not her husband. It was more than complicated.

Jesus met her in the middle of her mess. No mess would have been big enough to deter Him. He didn't need her to explain her broken relationships. He already knew those details. He gently pursued her heart, longing to win her trust.

Suddenly uncomfortable with feeling so exposed, she tried to change the subject. Perceiving Jesus to be a prophet, she asked Him about proper worship:

"Our fathers worshiped on this mountain, but you (Jews) say that in Jerusalem is the place where people ought to worship. I know that Messiah is coming, He who is called Christ. When He comes, He will tell us all things."[13]

Kindly and patiently, Jesus continued to speak truth to her. He wanted her to understand Who He was, to reach for the lasting solutions only He could offer her:

True worship is not in a place, but in a Person.
True living water is not from the earth,
but from the Maker of heaven and earth.
The true Messiah does make all things clear and right
and she no longer needed to wait to meet Him.
He was standing right in front of her.
Placing her trust in the true Messiah would change everything.

Jesus met her questions. But He never let the broken parts of her story be forgotten. He was effectively saying "I know your story and My offer of living water, of a changed, eternal life, still stands. Your story is *why* My offer stands." He knew He was the only One who could rescue her and He wanted her to know that too. He drew her heart to reach for Him and to experience true and lasting deliverance!

We simply know this dear lady as the woman at Sychar's well.

She may have been on the wrong side of town with a whole host of bad life choices, but JESUS saw beyond all the exterior details and reached her heart! She was watching for the Messiah who would tell her all things. Although she didn't fully understand, she knew there was something wondrous about this Man at the well and she couldn't wait to tell anyone who would listen that she believed the Messiah was here!

She left her water pot and went straight into the center of town. She had a new story to tell and it had nothing to do with her and everything to do with her Savior!

He had overwhelmed her heart with truth and pointed her to eternal life and she couldn't wait to share it. "Come and See!!!"[14] excitedly spilled from her lips as she met one face after another with urgency. And those people who probably hadn't paid much attention to her in the past? They were captivated by her news— and they came! They confidently proclaimed:

"We know that He is indeed the Savior of the world."

John 4:42 (ESV)

୫ . ୬

This is our GOD—He draws people to Himself. He opens our eyes to understand who we are and who He is, that aligning ourselves with the one true GOD is our best and only answer.

Our Savior doesn't just meet our need, check the box and move on to the next person. An impersonal provision of redemption and security is not what He has in mind. He wants to reach our hearts.

He impacts individuals with human touch and words of truth, unshakable reason to hope, and deep healing that is life changing. He transforms the broken parts of our stories in such a way that we cannot keep it to ourselves—because those who know grace cannot be silent! Our testimonies of His mercy are so powerful that others cannot help but take notice and want to know more!

Those who look to Him for help will be radiant with joy; no shadow of shame will darken their faces.

Psalm 34:5

℘ . ℭ

Read more of their stories . . . and reflect on your own!

RAHAB
Joshua 2:1–2:4, 6:22–25, Hebrews 1:31

When we are first introduced to Rahab, what did she know/believe about Israel's GOD?

What was her greatest fear?

In what ways did she demonstrate courageous faith?

How did GOD respond to, and then alter her story?

THE WOMAN AT SYCHAR'S WELL
John 4

What was the Samaritan woman's greatest hope?

How was JESUS' interaction with her unique?

What did the LORD want her to know about Him?

How did the LORD use her story to draw others to Him?

OVERALL

If JESUS met you face to face in your daily grind today, what questions might He have for you?

What broken parts of your story might He want to touch so He could bring healing?

What would it mean to you to know that He purposely detours right into your path to have personal encounters with you?

What does He want you to understand about yourself or about Him (or both!) that could bring restoration and align your heart with the One who longs to write the rest of your story?

ဢ . ဿ

Who is this One we are getting to know more intimately? The LORD revealed Himself to Rahab and the Samaritan woman as:

★ the One who is Maker of heaven and earth
★ the One who is our Savior
★ the One who uses dire circumstances to draw our hearts to Him

- ★ the One who goes out of His way to find us
- ★ the One who changes lives, offers new life!
- ★ the One who not only values us, He LOVES us!
- ★ the One who is not deterred by the broken parts of our story
- ★ the One who simply wants us to place our trust in Him
- ★ the One who gives us a new story to tell!

Chapter Four

the *One* who can be trusted: blessed is she who experiences His limitlessness

*I*t was a long, hard road that brought us to an unexpected future. We both knew what it was like to be alone, suddenly single again—and worse. We had lived the harsh reality of being rejected, cast aside, abandoned while our previous spouses pursued other relationships, and left to wonder if it was too late or too impossible to know the joy of a GOD-honoring marriage.

But GOD. How gracious is He? It is still staggering to realize He had other plans, set in motion long before I had the heart to receive them . . .

We were both seniors in high school, living in the suburbs of Philadelphia. I attended a big public high school northwest of the city. He attended a small private Christian school on the southwest side. Our church picnic every June was on the grounds of that same Christian school, so I knew his campus well. One of my closest friends from church was a member of his graduating class of about fifty. I attended their senior dinner and was present at his graduation. But we never met. Not then. Not on any of those occasions.

While he went to college in Boston, I attended the University of Delaware, very close to his home in southeastern Pennsylvania. I considered visiting his church in Wilmington, Delaware, many times—but never went. His sisters came to a Bible conference at my church more than once—but he never came. There were so many times that we could have met, times that we might have considered to be perfectly orchestrated by GOD to bring us together. But we didn't. Because GOD's perfect timing was so different.

In the years before we met, the LORD walked each of us through experiences that touched us deeply, broke our hearts but realigned our thinking, and drew us closer to Him first. He used those years to position our hearts to truly value and treasure one another. In His divine plan, it was ten more years before He caused our paths to meet. Ten years after first thinking of visiting Brandywine Chapel, I finally stepped inside those doors.

He would say that he knew the first day we met that he wanted to marry me. Haunted by heartache, I was the harder one to convince! But he patiently waited three more years while the LORD continued to heal my heart and open my eyes to just how attractive a heart for GOD can be! By the time I realized that the LORD was bringing us together with a beautiful future in mind, he was graduating from law school and we were both ready to take an exciting step forward—together.

As I slipped my arm into his on our wedding day, I remember feeling a peace and wholeness I had never known. Our gracious GOD reached beyond our perceived limitations and orchestrated our beautiful day. Time seemed to stand still as we basked in the tenderness of His arms around us.

Praise to the Lord, Who o'er all things so wondrously reigneth, shelters thee under His wings, yea, so gently sustaineth! Hast thou not seen how thy desires e'er have been granted in what He ordaineth?

Words based on Psalm 103, by
Joachim Neander, 1680

ಬ . ೮೪

Two women in desperate need of the Savior had the chance to cross paths with Him, GOD in the flesh, on the very same day. They both needed Him at exactly the same time, in different ways and in different locations. Both probably felt it was "now or never"—if *He* couldn't step in right then and there, it would be too late! How did JESUS make the excruciating choice between two people in need?

[spoiler alert] He didn't have to!

A dear bleeding woman had been suffering. For a long time! She had been held captive by disease's hold on her natural body for twelve years. She was weary from exhausting every possible channel to find healing. And then, she had the chance to be within arm's reach of the Savior, *her* Savior!

She pushed through the crowds. Because of her condition, she had been ostracized, prohibited from coming within reach of anyone. Others feared that, by law, her bleeding would defile them. Suddenly, none of that mattered. She charged forward, propelled by a single thought, "if I can just touch His clothing, I will be healed."[15]

JESUS didn't let her down! He was not satisfied with simply healing through her faith-filled touch of His garment. He wanted so much more for her. He immediately perceived "that power had gone out from Him"[16] and stopped to ask who had touched Him. JESUS wanted her to see Him face to face, to feel His touch, to look into His eyes, to hear Him call her "daughter"[17] —and to know, really know that her faith *in Him* had saved her, to hear directly from Him that she would experience peace and wholeness she had never known.

Scripture's descriptive account transports us to that busy street, not unlike our rushed life now. The same LORD JESUS, who wasn't satisfied with an impersonal dispatch of healing power, reaches to us individually and personally as well. He who is the same yesterday, today and forever still cares enough to make time and commitments stand still long enough to make sure we see Him, feel His touch and hear His words claiming us as His own.

What perceived hurdles are we willing to push through to allow a personal encounter with JESUS to happen? He offers His reassurance that our utter, unshakable confidence in Him is never displaced and will never let us down!

> *Praise the Lord, O my soul, and forget not ... the One who heals all your diseases.*
>
> Psalm 103:2,3 (NIV)

Then there was Jairus's daughter. In desperation, a synagogue leader named Jairus found JESUS, who agreed to go home with him to touch and heal his daughter. It was on their way, and despite their singular-focused urgency, that this woman, sick as long as his daughter had been alive, reached out in her own desperation to touch JESUS' garment and was healed. Jairus' anxiety mounted as JESUS stopped to meet her and interact with her in a meaningful and life-changing way.

In that moment, Jairus' worst fears seemed to come true. It was too late! A member of his household arrived to tell him that his daughter had just died. He would never deny this poor woman her personal encounter with the Savior, but the questions swirled and raged—did it have to be at the cost of his daughter's life?

When I read what JESUS said to him, I picture Him taking Jairus by the shoulders (both of them!), turning him to meet JESUS' gaze, squarely and unavoidably, blocking out any other sight or sound, saying,

"Don't be afraid, just trust Me."

Mark 5:36

I can only imagine that JESUS said those words with convincing authority. Gently, but powerfully. Jairus' head must have still been spinning, his heart pounding, but he responded with enough belief to lead JESUS home to his daughter. His courageous faith enabled him to witness and live the impossible!

The One who breathed life into his daughter the moment her life was conceived was the same One who breathed new life into her once more. Jairus' daughter opened her eyes, got up from her death bed and joined her jubilant parents in having something to eat!

Jairus experienced the reality that JESUS, our Savior, is never limited. And with Him, it is never too late! CHRIST's provision for one person never cancels out His perfect plan for someone else. This is our Savior. He is perfectly all-sufficient for each and every one of us. We can trust Him!

Praise the Lord, O my soul, and forget not... the One who renews your youth like the eagle's.

Psalm 103:2,5 (NIV)

80 . CR

Life was cozy raising two young children in quaint, small-town Pennsylvania. My husband's office was a stroller walk away. Kind neighbors sweetened our days with fresh cookies, smiles and conversation. Playgroup moms surrounded and strengthened me in those early days as a new mom. The back yard of our little red-brick house was encircled by a quintessential white picket fence and Pennsylvanian candle lights set the windows aglow each night.

I often expressed my gratitude to the LORD for His many blessings by saying it would take a lot to pull me out of that place!

But GOD. He loves us too much to leave us content with our perceptions of what is best. He needed me to know that His plans and purposes were not limited to *that* place. He longed to reveal His heart to me—that His best is not in a place, but in His Person.

My husband sensed His clear direction, but again, I was the harder one to convince.

The LORD unexpectedly and dramatically moved in my husband's professional life, directing us away from that place that felt so much like "home." He was gentle, but persistent, pointing much farther south than I ever would have considered—to Savannah, Georgia. My husband was excited. But I was kicking and screaming. Fear and uncertainty hung like a heavy cloud.

My husband's interview trip to Savannah loomed. Despite my honest struggle with this potential path, I did not want him to board that plane feeling abandoned, left alone in the pursuit of GOD's perfect plan for us.

I wrestled with the LORD for over a week. There were tears. Prayers. Hard questions. Why? Why couldn't we just stay where we were? We loved our home, our town, our community, and the relatively short drive to gather with family near Philadelphia. In just a few years, our hearts were already knit to so many dear friends. We were raising littles together, wrestling truth, sharing coffee, and rejoicing in GOD's goodness. Was He really asking me to give it all up?

The unknown was so very scary! Although I had heard and

seen truly lovely things about Savannah, it was too. far. away! And completely unfamiliar. No. I didn't want to go. I just didn't!

But GOD. Slowly, over days of pouring out my anxieties to Him, He touched and opened my heart. Instead of fearing the unknown, I began to realize the beauty of this man the LORD had given to lead me forward. I would have happily lived and died in the same house! But, because of my sweet and courageous husband, our little family would be able to experience things we never would have known if it were all up to me.

GOD's perfect plan unfolding in my husband's heart was never intended to cancel out His best for me. We are one. He will only direct what is truly best for both of us—what will reveal His heart to each member of our family in fresh, new ways. His best *is* truly best, for all of us.

Before he packed his bags to fly south, I could honestly say I shared my husband's joy-filled anticipation. The LORD had changed my heart. He simply asked me, *"Are you willing to trust Me? Trust that I will lead your family through this man I have called to protect and provide for you?"* As a gracious Father, He reminded me Who He is and to whom I belong. His loving kindness and truth quieted my anxious questions. I could only reply, *"Yes, LORD. I will trust You!"*

When GOD confirmed His direction to move to Savannah, we chose to follow, without fully knowing, but trusting the One who can be trusted!

Praise the Lord, O my soul, and forget not... the One who satisfies your desires with good things.

Psalm 103:2,5 (NIV)

· ℭ

Two other women in desperate need. The ache of each of their hearts was unique. But the source of their only hope for rescue was the same. The living GOD. He heard the cries of their hearts and used His prophet Elisha to expand their understanding of His power—and His loving care for them.

One dear woman was alone and afraid. Her husband, a prophet who had faithfully served the LORD, had just died. With little means to support herself, creditors threatened to enslave her two sons. She could not bear the thought of losing them too!

Elisha asked what she had in the house. She answered honestly—there was nothing except a little bit of oil. Upon Elisha's direction, she borrowed as many empty containers as they could gather from neighbors and began pouring from that one little flask. Miraculously, oil continued to flow until all available containers were filled to the brim. The sale of the oil provided the means for them to satisfy their creditors and live comfortably without fear of debt.

We don't know how long they struggled with rising fear in their doubt-filled situation. Sometimes the LORD allows those trials to linger, so we know the depths of that hunger, the very real ache for a rescue only He can provide. The LORD's directions through Elisha were simple, uncomplicated, and involved the whole family.

GOD met them at the height of their crisis and cared for them. He stretched the known physical limits to provide for their needs and protect the unity of their home.

Then there was a sweet and thoughtful woman from Shunem. In his travels, Elisha often stopped at their home to enjoy a meal. She and her husband built an extra room on their roof to provide overnight lodging for him.

She did not look for anything in return. It was her joy to show him hospitality and to support his work for the LORD. When asked, she humbly replied that she was content, in need of nothing.

But the LORD knew her heart, her longing for a son. Through Elisha, He promised that she would bear a son within the next year. Her elation was guarded. Should she even dare to hope?

The LORD fulfilled His promise. Although her husband was advanced in years, this sweet woman now knew the joy of motherhood!

Until...

The torturous day came when her son fell ill and died. It all happened so quickly. She couldn't even speak. With her husband still busy with the reapers in the field, she laid her son on Elisha's bed and saddled a donkey to go straight to Elisha.

She fell down before him, wracked with grief. "Didn't I tell you not to raise my hopes?"[18] Her only tangible link to the living GOD, she clung to Elisha. She would not leave him, so he followed her home.

Her mind swirled. Surely it was already too late. Her son had died! Still moving in a daze, she led Elisha to his own room where the boy lay, and left him alone, closing the door.

She sat and stared, not knowing how to process all that had happened. How did a morning that seemed so normal end in this grip of death? She heard praying. And pacing. And more praying. Commotion she couldn't distinguish.

And then, seven little sneezes. The door burst open and she was called to come see and embrace her son—alive!

For the heart of a mother, there is no greater fear than losing her child. The LORD used Elisha to meet each of these women in that terrifying place. Both women held onto a spark of hope. They knew Who to turn to! They had seen the power of GOD working miracles in other's lives and believed He could do the same for them.

Fear and desperation can engulf us like a flood! How many times has this same question haunted our thoughts: "I know GOD is good. But will He be good to me?!" To believe otherwise is contrary to all we know of the heart of GOD. Neither of these women fully understood the reasons for their trials. They didn't know what to do next. But they knew Who to ask! They held onto what they *did* know about the one true GOD and trusted Him to respond to their needs.

Our GOD values our devotion to Him. Our choice to trust Him. He is the only One who is able! To do anything. At any time. What we think is "final" is not final to Him. What we consider a dead-end is an abundant opportunity for Him to demonstrate His power. He makes a way when there seems to be no way! He provides what we don't even dare to hope for. He is the One who is never limited. And never too late!

> *Praise the Lord, O my soul, and forget not... the One who redeems your life and crowns you with love and compassion.*

Psalm 103:2,4 (NIV)

℞ . ℟

One day. We had one, whirlwind, jam-packed schedule kind of day to tour an unthinkable number of houses with a realtor and secure a "landing pad" for our family in Savannah. Take-off from north central Pennsylvania was in the dark hours of the morning to ensure that we would arrive in Georgia early enough to meet the realtor by nine o'clock.

My head and heart were a swirl of excitement, questions, and the myriad details of the different homes we had selected online for this one-day search. My type-A self was in full-tilt, sure that I would need my head on straight, sorting details and feeling especially decisive. As we began our descent, the pilot interrupted my self-pep talk.

An unexpected storm had covered the sky with thick menacing clouds. After circling a few times, hoping the skies would clear, we were in danger of being re-routed to Jacksonville, Florida.

I was stunned. My heart raced and pounded. Hot tears started to brim as I felt "our" plan for this day slipping from our grasp. Old doubts surfaced. Why? Why did we have to leave where we were? Why did I get my hopes up, thinking we could be brave enough to step boldly forward? Didn't I say this would be too hard, too complicated? This long-distance move felt overwhelming—and impossible!

But GOD. How gracious is He? His Spirit grabbed my thoughts and held them captive when I was incapable of wrangling them. It could only have been His prompting that led my shift in prayer:

"LORD, please give me grace! If You have a completely different plan for this day, grant me the ability to receive it from Your hand, to see what next step we should take, and to trust You have all the details worked out in ways I could never imagine. ... But, You are GOD! It is within Your power to move these clouds so we can land! Help me trust Your wisdom...."

Literally as the thoughts were still rising from my heart, the pilot interrupted again. Inexplicably, the skies had opened just enough. We had been given clearance from the tower to land in Savannah, on time!

Tears welled up in stunned awe and deep appreciation. I could not believe the LORD heard my prayers and was delighted to meet my ten seconds of courageous faith to demonstrate that He is sovereign.

As we exited the plane, thanking the crew for their faithful service, someone mentioned an interesting update from the tower. Immediately following our successful landing, the skies thickened and threatened once again. All other flights were, in fact, redirected to neighboring cities. Ours was the only plane to land that morning.

We made it! By His strength we powered through more house tours in one day than most humans should ever attempt and shook our heads with a knowing laugh as we collapsed into our hotel bed that night. None of the houses we saw that day were the home for us. But while driving through a new neighborhood near brand new primary and elementary schools, we discovered a spacious lot, a favorite layout and a builder who would construct our new home!

Only GOD. Only the living GOD is powerful enough to command the creation He spoke into existence. Only our gracious Father is loving enough to value the needs of a single day in our humble life—and provide for us above and beyond any expectation. Only our Savior delights to meet our trust in Him with a glimpse of glory!

$$\infty . \text{CB}$$

We had not faced the loss of a child, a serious financial crisis, a chronic disease draining strength or hope or resources over long, hard years. But the LORD used the challenges we faced to show us Who He is—the One who is not bound by any limitation, the One who is trustworthy!

In big and little ways, GOD cared for our young family. He stretched the known physical limits to provide for our needs and point us to our new home.

This is our Savior. He is perfectly all-sufficient for each and every one of us. He is never limited. And never too late! We can trust Him. He wants us to know, to really know that He hears the cries of our hearts. That faith *in Him* will lead us to peace and wholeness we have never known.

Now glory be to God! By His mighty power at work within us, He is able to accomplish infinitely more than we would ever dare to ask or hope.

⁓ . ⁓

Read more of their stories . . . and reflect on your own!

THE POOR WIDOW & THE SHUNAMITE
2 Kings 4:1–36

When Elisha encountered these two women, what were their needs?

How did the LORD stretch the known perceptions of what was possible to meet their needs?

What were their greatest fears?

What did they learn about GOD?

What did He want them to know about His heart?

What does the LORD value?

THE BLEEDING WOMAN & JAIRUS' DAUGHTER
Mark 5:21–43

When JESUS encounters this woman and a young girl needing His help so desperately at exactly the same time, how does He choose?

Held and Beloved – 47

What limitations did each face?

How did JESUS respond to each?

How did He address the woman, and the girl's father?

What words of JESUS brought comfort, calm, courage or healing?

What did JESUS reveal about Himself through their stories?

OVERALL

What are the cries of your heart today?

What verses from GOD's Word reassure you that He hears you?

With what "impossible" is the LORD asking you to trust Him?

What perceived limitation haunts your mind and steals peace from your heart?

What fresh truth about the heart of GOD might bring healing and wholeness you didn't think possible?

ⅎ . ⅓

Who is this One we are getting to know more intimately? The LORD revealed Himself to the poor widow & the Shunamite and to the bleeding woman & Jairus and his daughter as:

* the One who knows and cares about our needs
* the One who interacts with us personally
* the One who is able to do anything at any time
* the One whose best for one never cancels out His best for someone else

* the One who gives us simple instructions
* the One who is faithful to His promises
* the One who is good—to us!
* the One who gives us reason to HOPE!

Chapter Five

the One who leads me through the storm: blessed is she who steps out with courage

A young girl named Esther was surrounded by opulence beyond her imagination, catered to at every turn with the finest of offerings, in a swirl of people, excitement, anticipation, and wonder.

But she never felt more alone.

Her losses compounded and her heart broke.

Bereft of her parents and her homeland, now she was also grieving the loss of the one person she could still claim as family and the humble place she had embraced as home. They, too, had been taken away.

It all happened so fast. A shocking announcement from the palace in the land of Persia, where her people, the Israelites, had been exiled. Rumors of an edict from King Ahasuerus's court that he was looking for a new queen quickly grew into harsh reality. Esther was collected along with all other girls her age. Each of them would be presented to the king, for him to choose which young virgin pleased him most.

There was barely time to process, or plan, or gather her thoughts for any final words in the rushed goodbye. Mordecai, her older cousin who had faithfully cared for her and raised her as his own daughter, made one thing crystal clear. "*Do not* reveal your heritage. *Do not* let them know to Whom you belong."[19]

It was his bold attempt to protect her. From misjudgment? From mistreatment? Worse? His wild eyes shot fear through her heart. What was she about to experience?

The response of the other girls stretched the gamut. Sadness. Fear. Uncertainty. Unhappiness. Blank stares of shock. Thrill. Wonder. Anticipation. Competition. It was all very overwhelming.

Now on the palace grounds, Esther was less fearful. Many of the unknowns melted into a less frightening reality. But her heart still broke. The overriding weight was haunting loneliness.

No one knew her. No one understood her. No one could even be told where she was from, what she valued, what she truly felt. Everything was strange. Unfamiliar. And there were still intimidating unknowns about what would be expected of her.

Then the surprising news arrived. Esther had been chosen. Chosen? What exactly did that mean?

The genuineness of Esther's character had won the hearts of so many around her. And now the heart of the king. He had chosen her to be his new queen! A new flood of ceremonies, festivities, customs, preparations, and expectations swept her along as one day bled into the next. What did she think? How did she feel? Was there anyone in whom she could confide as she scrambled to process it all?

Her life seemed desperately out of control, so vastly different than anything she had ever dreamed about. And still, in the sea of people and activity, she felt so isolated and alone.

What could be the purpose in this hugely unthinkable course of events. Why? Why her? What exactly was she supposed to be doing in that place?

Slowly, she was beginning to adjust to her new surroundings, new routines, just doing the next thing, trusting that one day it would all be clear. Then, another shocking announcement from the palace. Devastating. Horrifying. Her people, whom she had never felt free to acknowledge, were in grave danger!

Her cousin Mordecai managed to send a message to her. A challenge she needed to read several times to take in. He directed her to go before King Ahasuerus and plead for the lives of her people! Uninvited, this would be a risky endeavor. Life-threateningly risky!

Mordecai had strongly advised Esther never to reveal her heritage. He worked so hard to protect her. But now. Everything was different. Her people were in danger and he was convinced she would not be spared. Quite the contrary, he believed that she was perfectly placed for this exact purpose. Only *she* was in the position to pursue a private audience with the king and the attention of his heart to bring about an otherwise impossible rescue.

New fears. New unknowns. Complete and utter uncertainty. But the lives of her people were at stake. GOD's people. If He had purposely placed her to stand in the gap, she would turn to Him for courage to step forward.

Esther asked Mordecai to gather everyone to fast and pray for three days. She and the women closest to her would do the same. Her heart raced as she dressed and prepared to approach the throne. With final prayers and a deep breath, she fixed her eyes on the king and awaited her fate.

King Ahasuerus raised the golden scepter! And welcomed Esther to his side. This meant she would not lose her life for approaching the king uninvited. The next two days sped into motion. The king responded to her generous hospitality, her bold request to host a banquet for him and Haman, his highest court official. Two days in a row.

The king perceived that Esther was concerned about more than a fancy dinner. On both occasions, he asked her to tell him the true purpose of their time together. On the second evening, she gathered the courage to reveal the cry of her heart—the lives of her people! Shocked and horrified, King Ahasuerus demanded to know who would do such a thing, to place her and her people in such grave danger!? Esther bravely pointed to Haman and revealed that he was the mastermind of the destructive edict.

The king's actions were immediate and decisive. The enemy of God's people was destroyed and the edict for their annihilation over-written!

The one true God in whom she placed her trust granted His people victory! The heathen king to whom she was now married embraced Esther and her people and protected them. Although He was never mentioned by Name, God was always present and His hand was always working behind the scenes to bring redemption and security that was undeniably from Him.

After so many heart-wrenching losses and unanswered questions, Esther could testify with confidence. The living God had a specific plan to rescue His people. The One whom she trusted had knowingly sent her into the middle of a heathen palace, into scary and terrifyingly unfamiliar unknowns. He asked her to endure losses that touched her deeply. But He never left her side. She was never alone. He heard her cries and the longings of her heart. He honored her reach for Him with the courage to believe she was perfectly placed to step out in courage at just the right time.

God knowingly called Esther into the middle of a "storm." In that place, He knew she would understand with certainty that He was with her, that prayer is powerful, and that He is sovereign!

Perhaps you were made queen for just such a time as this!

Esther 4:14

Despite my fears, trepidations, and out-right resistance, the LORD was gracious. He proved again and again that the same loving Hand that had pieced together such a cozy life for us in small-town Pennsylvania was willing and able to do it again in Savannah!

Our "window in the clouds" had led us to a home in a developing area just south of the city. It was a sweet, family friendly place with a large military community and big hearts. A chapel on the grounds of a Bible camp in the middle of the marsh became our church home and its dear people welcomed us as long-lost family. Life was rich and full, quaint and lovely, and close to home. Our only ventures outside of a five to ten-mile radius were to visit the picturesque squares, riverfront, and tea rooms in downtown Savannah, or to stroll the beaches on Tybee Island.

We quickly adopted many sweetly southern pastimes like bare feet, peaches, sweeter-than-sweet tea, and generous hospitality. And carried with us some northern touches like candle lights in the windows and the love of a crisp clear day that welcomed a glowing fireplace! Much to their disappointment and horror, our new friends never did convince us that boiled peanuts were anything close to a delicacy or that the beauties of that place outweighed the battle with sand gnats. But we carved out a home there. We counted our abundant blessings often and eagerly invited others to visit and bask in our sweetly southern existence.

In moments of reflection, we could surmise some of the purposes in the LORD leading us to our new home—the lessons He planned to teach us as well as the ways He wanted to use us in that place. Despite the immovable distance from favorite faces and places in the northern hills, I truly treasured our home in Savannah as a bountiful gift from the LORD.

But GOD.

He was about to take my heart to a deeper level of a familiar lesson. He knew I still didn't fully understand that He loves us too much to leave us content in our own perceptions of what is best.

Again, He began stirring my husband's heart, and moving in his professional life. Again, He was asking us to step forward with courage. This time even farther south. To south Florida!

We had seen the LORD direct our first move. We had already learned not to confine Him or His plans within a box of our own making. For a second time, He made His direction clear and firm to us. Knowing we were able to trust Him with our first move south, we stepped bravely forward, believing we could trust Him again.

Our faith was properly founded. The truth of GOD's faithfulness remained. But trying to adjust to another new place seemed too much for my fragile heart.

Unlike Savannah, there was little about south Florida that appealed to me. It felt like a completely different world. A world where others were not unkind, but seemingly unaware, content to operate solely within their own bubble of existence. Interaction seemed impossible, making it very difficult to meet people or build new relationships. I missed the joys of living in a small town. Our second new home felt foreign and cold, strange and unwelcoming. I was homesick, not necessarily for Savannah (although that was the most recent home we knew and loved), but for anywhere that would feel more like "us!" I was longing for the settled feeling of being able to stay in one place for more than a few years.

Old wounds re-opened. Old doubts and questions raged. Again, I was in a deep wrestle with the LORD.

Why did He bring us here? Why couldn't we stay where we were? He knew how difficult this would be and yet He confidently made His direction known to us. How? Why? I had days of bitter grief, confusion, swirling questions, heartbreak, and even anger. I really didn't mean to be rebellious. I simply couldn't see any clear vision of what I was supposed to be doing in this strange, new place! I pleaded with the LORD to show me the next step to take and all I could see was fog.

My poor husband did not know what to do for me. Even though I kept a good bit of my thoughts and struggles from him, he saw right through my attempts to be strong and grieved with me. At one point, he dared to ask, "Was I wrong? Was this not the move we were supposed to make?" But we both kept coming back to the confidence we felt in hearing and seeing the LORD lead us here, much like He had confirmed our first move south. We both remembered seeing and knowing the obvious challenges we would face here as opposed to Savannah. And yet we were willing to brave it, trusting the LORD had a purpose and a plan. Those challenges were much more difficult in "real time."

BUT... ah, that glorious word "BUT." I am thrilled to say that the story did not end there! Even on my toughest days, I would repeat scripture to myself and remind myself often, "He is faithful." He always had been, and I knew He would be again, even if I couldn't see how. As He had done so many times before, He slowly, patiently worked on my heart to teach me new things. I experienced serious growing pains, but I don't regret one tear-stained moment.

Knowing the LORD could use His word to powerfully shift my heart, I became hungry to hear as much as possible from Him. Lessons from Matthew 11:28–30 became very precious to me:

> *Come to Me, all who are weary and carry heavy burdens, and I will give you rest. Take My yoke upon you. Let Me teach you, because I am humble and gentle, and you will find rest for your souls. For My yoke fits*

perfectly, and the burden I give you is light.

Let Him carry my burdens. Learn from Him. Find rest.

Was I willing to be in the trenches with Him? Learn things by His side that I would not learn any other way? Was I willing to admit that it is only the things that touch us deeply that will change us forever? That it is only when we are struggling so severely that we *need* and come to recognize the reality of His presence and His heart speaking to ours?

This season in my life began to make a little more sense. It was so much less about what I was supposed to be *doing* and so much more about embracing the opportunity to be alone with the LORD and to be learning and resting.

Several months into this difficult transition, my husband and I had the opportunity to attend a concert. A relatively new artist, Lindsay McCaul, opened the evening with her song, "Take My Hand." Tears welled up as I recognized the cry of my heart over recent months. The song is about the LORD calling to Peter in the boat, bidding him come to Him on the water:

I heard You say it, I know You did / You called me out into the waves and wind / and for a moment I was brave and strong / but now everything is going wrong / didn't You know that I'd be scared / couldn't You see I was unprepared / I'm not asking for

*reasons You hold or the safety of land
/ I just need You to take my hand*

- Lindsay McCaul -

The Father knew the challenges I was going to face and yet He lovingly called me into the storm, knowing the result would be an amazing opportunity for Him to reveal more of His heart to me. I didn't need Him to stop the storm or coddle me and let me stay in the boat. I just needed Him to take my hand and *I needed Him to help me* reach for His. I didn't need to have it all figured out, I just needed to step out in courageous faith, one moment at a time.

Just when I thought the trial was behind me, there was one more, completely unexpected challenge. It came in the thick of house-hunting for a more permanent home in south Florida, one we could buy rather than rent. Again, we had tackled more house tours than any human should attempt. But before long, we were confident we had found the one that was intended for us.

The day before we were to sign the offer, I completely fell apart. I was a bundle of emotions and fear and raging resistance, "I *don't* want to buy a house here, I *don't* want to stay here, I can't do this anymore, it's just too hard!" I sobbed like a baby and brought a stop to the whole process. My husband wasn't about to move forward unless we were both confident and I was anything but.

All night I tossed and turned, wondering where this relapse had come from. What did it all mean? How could I feel so scared that I wasn't making sense, to myself or anyone else? My thoughts drifted back to the yoke in Matthew. His Spirit whispered to my heart:

"We're in this together, and we can hang out in this pause as long as you're comfortable, but neither of us can accomplish anything more until we move FORWARD. We're yoked together. I can't move until you are willing to take that step with Me."

Morning dawned with renewed confidence to throw caution and senseless emotion to the wind and boldly move ahead with our offer. To get settled and watch the LORD unfold what He had planned for us in our second new home. A timely message from my sister that very morning gave me the "kick in the pants" only a sister can give: "It's time to move forward, not back! Buy the house, get settled and get to work! This is where the LORD has placed you and you have work to do, so get busy and stop feeling sorry for yourself!" I could only smile through tears of confirmation. I knew the wrestling through the night had brought me to the right conclusion.

By the end of our first year in south Florida, a lot of the heartache had melted away and we could only see His faithful leading, guiding, and providing hand. From time to time, I still had questions with few answers, still felt like a fish out of water, still longed for a place that felt more like "home." But I found rest in a few overwhelming truths. The living GOD longs for us to know Him more intimately. He longs for us to understand the immensity of His love for us—as well as our utter dependence upon Him.

Our Savior is willing to call us into whatever storm is necessary to reveal Himself to us. In that place, He knows we will understand with certainty that His love surrounds us, His truth steadies us, and His Spirit gives us courage to reach through the fog for His hand.

Be strong and courageous... for the Lord your God will be with you wherever you go.

Joshua 1:9

A young girl was chosen for an unexpected role. Called to walk a path few understood.

She was relatively unknown, possibly as young as fourteen when she learned that she'd been chosen. Like Esther, she was purposely placed to step out in courage as GOD's eternal plan of redemption for His people unfolded.

Her name was Mary. We aren't even given a last name, simply that she was from Nazareth. She was chosen by GOD to carry, birth, and raise the LORD JESUS, fully Man yet always Divine, the Son of the Most High GOD.

Her role was honored and important, mightily blessed, yet incredibly challenging. She knew the power and presence of the Holy Spirit long before the early believers at Pentecost. It was His Spirit that overshadowed her when the LORD JESUS entered her body as an unborn Baby. But her calling would be carried out in largely unseen, private, simply faithful and steadfast moments in a humble home.

What can we learn about GOD from her story? How can I see His hand working through her experiences and answer His call on my own life as I ponder hers? There are many intricate details that captivate my attention. But I find myself lingering over some of the more difficult moments she faced.

Mary was the only person present at both the LORD's birth and His death. Mary was the one who probably spent the most time with JESUS. Face to face, in conversation, physically touched and impacted by Him in so many ways for more than thirty years.

We are given so few glimpses into that relationship, those day-to-day interactions. Could the LORD have chosen to record very little about their intimate moments because each of us has our own intensely personal connection with our Savior that the details of His relationship with Mary are appropriately private, above and beyond any possible comparison?

Scripture tells us that Mary treasured all these things in her heart. Not shared, not boasted about, not questioned. No. She simply valued all those moments—some private, some public—all her observations of this remarkable Child growing into a Man.

Mary listened to His words and pondered them. She learned to trust in this God Man she was getting to know so intimately. She trusted Him to make clear to her just what she needed to know when she needed to know it. She understood before He was even born that He came to be her Savior and humbly responded, "I am the Lord's servant."[20] She was confident that He would provide for her every need. Always. Perfectly.

It is difficult to linger over thoughts about Mary at the foot of the cross, watching the brutal death of this One she raised. What depths of human emotions must have overwhelmed her! The physical and emotional torture He endured would have been excruciating enough to observe. The injustice of the whole scene must have made her insides burn and ache. But to add insult to injury, she was close enough to see and hear the Roman soldiers divide His garments and cast lots for one that was a single-woven piece. Possibly one she had made for Him? I can't begin to imagine the range or extent of emotions Mary battled that day.

When you pass through the waters, I will be with you; and through the rivers, they shall not overwhelm you... for I am the Lord, your God, your Savior... you are precious and honored in My sight and I love you.

Isaiah 43:2–4(ESV)

In passages about the Lord's death, we see Jesus coming close to His own mother. The words from Isaiah becoming real and tangible in those dark moments. We can imagine His eyes

Held and Beloved – 61

meeting hers, His heart deeply caring and providing for her, His love for her drowning out the horrific scene and causing her to fix her eyes only on *Him*.

I can only think, in that moment, JESUS quieted Mary's raging emotions with His love. He reassured her that He was still with her. He reminded her to trust that her worst nightmare would bring glorious redemption and unalterable, everlasting LIFE!

Chosen. Mary was chosen by GOD to fill this role. Excruciatingly difficult. Often isolated. Misunderstood. Unfamiliar and frightening. But her Savior was with her every step of that journey. She experienced the overshadowing of the Holy Spirit. She treasured His Words, willingly offered herself as His servant, and lifted her voice in praise to Him!

Sovereign GOD knowingly called Mary into the path of a storm, on more than one occasion. In that place, He knew she would notice and ponder truths about His plan and His love for her that would hold her together and give her courageous vision for the eternal future He secured.

The Lord your God is with you...
He will quiet you with His love.

Zephaniah 3:17 (ESV)

ᗬ . ᢁ

Read more of their stories . . . and reflect on your own!

ESTHER
Esther 1–10 (focus on Esther's personal experience)

As a young girl, what challenges did Esther face?

In what unusual (scary!) circumstances did she unexpectedly find herself?

When facing her greatest fears, what request did she make?

On whom did she depend for help?

How did the LORD use her unique position, time and place to alter her story and that of her people?

What did the LORD reveal about Himself to Esther?

MARY OF NAZARETH
Luke 1–2, John 2, John 19

As a young girl, what unique path did the LORD call her to walk?

What might have been the joys/challenges of her calling?

How did Mary respond to all that the LORD revealed to her heart?

What do we know about the intimate relationship between Mary and the LORD JESUS?

What might have been the darkest day for Mary? How might the LORD JESUS have come close to care for her personally in those hours?

OVERALL
Matthew 14:22–33 (the disciples on a stormy sea)

What do you observe and ponder as you get to know this One who has an unseen yet undeniable hand upon your life?

What causes you to treasure the unique and intensely personal relationship that is growing between you and your Savior?

Through what difficult days does He call you to walk?

How do you reach for Him through the fog? What encourages you to trust Him? Emboldens you to step forward with courage?

How differently might your circumstances appear if you search for His eyes, allow yourself to be captivated by His love and His power, to be quieted by His tender care and sovereign will?

What Scriptures speak truth that steadies your heart?

ᘒ . ᘓ

Who is this One we are getting to know more intimately? The LORD revealed Himself to Esther and Mary of Nazareth as:

* the One who knowingly calls us into the storm
* the One who is always with us
* the One to whom prayer is powerful
* the One who is Sovereign
* the One whose truth steadies us
* the One whose love surrounds us
* the One whose Spirit give us courage
* the One who gives us fresh vision for the future

Chapter Six

the *One* who grieves with me: blessed is she who opens her heart to be held

*I*t was just past seven in the morning when I slid behind the wheel to spell my husband who would be driving most of our trek home. A long day stretched ahead of us—sixteen more hours of the eighteen that would take us from the Pennsylvania hills to south Florida.

The sun was up but we still hadn't seen it. Honestly thankful for some cloud cover while driving through ninety-degree heat, I was grateful for a low-hung, misty morning. The envelope of cloud and drizzle seemed to hide me away as I wrestled a fresh round of bittersweet emotions.

The fog began to lift, giving a sneak peek of the stunning valleys as we cut our way through the mountains. I could see the higher peaks, standing tall and majestic in my rearview mirror. In the early morning light, they were the softest shade of lavender. With a car full of sleepers, I treasured this solitary moment to soak it all in as long as possible! I glanced toward the broadening expanse of sky in front of me and took a deep breath.

"LORD, You know my heart. You know how it breaks every time those northern hills are the ones we are leaving behind. But I open my hands to You, I open my heart to Your designs, I lift my eyes to the skies, and ask for one more reminder that Your thoughts are so much bigger than mine! Help me reach again for Your hand to lead us to the place You have for us."

This is not a new ache. Just twelve hours before, we lifted our voices in a wood and stone building in the middle of the woods to sing the opening hymn for an evening service of the family conference we had enjoyed for a week. I swallowed hard and tried to sing through the tears, and ended up only mouthing the words:

> *Stayed upon Jehovah, hearts are fully blessed, finding, as He promised, perfect peace and rest.*

Frances R. Havergal, 1876

His promises are true and faithful. They are. But sometimes, we need to be stayed by Him, because it is hard. In that moment, the tears welled up and the lump in my throat grew as I remembered a similar moment a decade before. We were days from leaving Pennsylvania, my home for thirty-seven years, to make the first of two difficult moves farther and farther south. I stood with dear friends to sing the opening hymn of our Bible Study Fellowship class. It was the last one I would attend in that place with those dear friends. I swallowed hard and tried to sing through the tears, but only mouthed the words:

> *what He says we will do, where He sends we will go... trust and obey, for*

there's no other way to be happy in Jesus,
but to trust and obey.

John H. Sammis, 1887

If I had known the years (years!) we would spend far from the only home I had ever known, I might have held on a little longer before we pulled out of town on that February day over a decade before. Years into that GOD-ordained journey, I still fight those tears and that mega-lump in my throat. But really, I can't help but smile too. That deep-down smile of the grateful and blessed. What a gift to have treasured faces and places that I still ache for after so many years!

The story we're living is that we had a stronger tug on our heart twelve years before and all the years since—to follow our Savior wherever He leads us. His best *is* best even when it breaks my heart and loss is real. I would choose all over again to love deep (deeply enough to really feel those losses), and to follow Him into the scary and unknown and often lonely. Again and again. For He is faithful. Always. And His purposes are exact and eternal!

The Lord makes firm the steps of
the one who delights in Him.

Psalm 37:23 (NIV)

Blessed are those who keep His
testimonies, who seek Him with their
whole heart.

Psalm 119:2 (ESV)

He also knows my heart. So, on that morning, driving south again with the northern hills behind me, He was so tender. I sensed His nearness, reassuring me. And when we crossed the border into Florida another twelve hours later, I caught sight of the setting sun dancing off the St. Mary's river in all its resplendence. He knows what will grab my attention, what will bring me a fresh wave of joy. It was beautiful. I was reminded that He is beautiful, and the place He called us to live is beautiful too!

I thanked Him for the extravagant gift of being able to travel back to the northern hills that have such a pull on my heart, for the two weeks we had spent there three summers in a row, and for the treasured times soaking in all those favorite faces and places! Despite the lump in my throat, I genuinely thanked Him for leading us so faithfully, for seeing us safely home to the space He had carved out for us in south Florida—eleven hundred miles from those northern hills! Loss is real, but there is so much more to gain when we choose Him.

And I prayed, *"May my Savior hold the strongest pull on my heart – always!"*

For the mountains may be removed and the hills may shake, but My loving kindness will not be removed from you. My covenant of peace will not be shaken, says the Lord who has compassion on you.

Isaiah 54:10 (NASB)

℘ . ℭ

LOSS. It was an ache Naomi and Ruth knew well. Painfully. Crushingly.

The LORD's best had become blurred for Naomi and her husband, Elimelech, in the challenges of famine. No bread in their homeland of Bethlehem. No income. Two growing boys. What choice did they have? They followed the only path that seemed possible, even though it led them away from the land of Judah. Away from the living GOD in whom they had always trusted. To the foreign land of Moab.

The harsh consequences of that choice seemed to string together to form one single word. L O S S.

The perceived provisions of that foreign land dwindled. A long, hard decade of years brought the loss of Naomi's husband and both of her sons. Bereft and hopeless, Naomi looked into the faces of her two daughters-in-law, now also widows, with dark, heavy eyes.

She had heard there was bread again in Bethlehem. That GOD had blessed and provided for His people. The trip would be long and sorrowful. But she decided it was her only wise choice—to go back.

Swallowed by grief and defeated by despair, Naomi tragically urged Ruth and Orpah to return to their families and homes, and to their lifeless gods. Her broken heart could not find the strength to encourage them to place their faith in the one true GOD she struggled to understand.

Orpah braved the harsh goodbye and returned home. But Ruth clung to Naomi, refusing to leave her side. Naomi counted her life too bitter to share, convinced the LORD's hand had turned against her. But, despite losing her husband and two sons, Naomi had gained a daughter. Flickering hope and courageous faith led Ruth to profess loyalty to Naomi, and more importantly, allegiance to the one true GOD!

Don't ask me to leave you and turn back. For wherever you go, I will go; wherever you live, I will live; Your people will be my people, and your God will be my God.

Ruth 1:16

The two women traveled the long road to Bethlehem together. One hollow with grief. The other rising above her own losses to look forward with hope, buoyed by young faith in the living GOD she had only begun to know.

When they reached Bethlehem, Naomi told the other women to call her "Mara."[21] In a single name, confessing the bitterness of her life of loss. But in His Word, the LORD never did. He knew the end of Naomi's story hadn't been revealed to her yet. He knew there was abundant, unexpected, who-would-ever-believe-it kind of joy waiting for her!

Sovereign GOD spoke through Naomi to direct Ruth into the care and provision of Boaz, a close relative who owned vast fields where wheat and barley were harvested. Even as a poor foreigner, Ruth was welcomed to follow along behind the reapers and gather whatever crops were left behind. Ruth worked hard, with humility and diligence, to provide food for herself and Naomi. Little did she know that Boaz would take notice of her. How kind and telling were Boaz's words to Ruth:

All that you have done for your mother-in-law since the death of your husband has been fully told to me, and how you left your father and mother and your native land and came to a people that you did not know before. The Lord repay you for what you have done, and a full reward be given you by the Lord, the God of Israel, under Whose wings you have come to take refuge!

Ruth 2:11-12 (ESV)

Ruth had come to the land of Israel as a foreigner, as a Moabite (shunned by the people of Israel). The "talk around town" could have been anything and everything unpleasant, prejudiced, misinterpreted, plain old made-up lies, and ugly gossip. But no! Boaz had never even met her, never spoken to her, but he knew a lot about her character.

She was devoted to her mother-in-law. She was hard working. She had left everything she knew to boldly claim Israel's GOD as her own. She was faithfully doing what the LORD had shown her to provide for herself and Naomi.

The humble display of Ruth's character, love and devotion to GOD must have been so striking that others couldn't help but comment about her in the highest regards. She simply remained faithful and let her character and her trust in the LORD's perfect provision speak for itself. Boaz saw those traits in her and valued them. The LORD was preparing his heart to step in as Ruth and Naomi's kinsman redeemer.

In the nation of Israel, when a man died, his closest male relative was called upon to purchase his land, to redeem it from foreclosure, and to maintain its possession within the family to whom it had been allotted when the Israelites entered the promised land during the days of Moses and Joshua. This near relative would also have the responsibility of marrying the man's widow, to bear a son who could carry on the deceased man's name, and eventually take ownership of the land that had been redeemed.

The LORD prompted Naomi's heart as well. She longed to find a more permanent home for Ruth. Naomi explained to Ruth that Boaz was in position to be their kinsman redeemer, and it was time to act on that provision. She gave Ruth specific instructions to bathe, put on perfume, dress in her nicest clothes, then go to the threshing floor where Boaz would be winnowing barley. Once he had finished eating and drinking and found a quiet place to lie down for the night, Ruth was directed to quietly lie at his feet and wait for him to tell her what to do next.

Ruth trusted Naomi. She followed her instructions exactly and courageously risked her reputation to go to Boaz, to pursue a private audience with him, to wait at his feet for him to welcome her request. When Boaz noticed her lying at his feet, he asked who she was. Ruth confidently but humbly answered, "I am your servant, spread the corner of your covering over me, for you are my family redeemer."[22]

Boaz received her warmly, blessed her and called her daughter. He was honored by her confidence in him to meet her needs and promised to pursue the process of redemption the very next morning. He arranged for Ruth to return to her mother-in-law under the cover of darkness and the strict confidence of anyone else present, thereby protecting her reputation. Boaz did not send her away empty handed. He piled barley so abundantly in her cloak that she struggled to carry it!

When Ruth reached home in the early morning hours, Naomi joyfully received the provision Boaz had sent and eagerly inquired about their time together at the threshing floor. When she heard of Boaz's kindness and promise to care for them, Naomi reassured Ruth's heart (with surprising strength growing inside her own), "be patient, my daughter, for the man will not rest until the matter is settled today."[23]

Naomi told Ruth to go, then she told her to wait, to be still and see how things would turn out. There was confidence and certainty about both directives. This is wisdom. This is our walk with the LORD. When He says go, we go. When He is working behind the scenes, He often asks us to wait, to be still until He call us to act again.

The LORD JESUS modelled this for us. Even being fully GOD, He never operated in isolation from the Father, but always in submission to Him, under His direction, committed to His sovereign plan and perfect timing. For everything. The Son trusted the Father implicitly. So can we. He is trustworthy. Restraint is not easy. But surrendering to the One who always finishes our story in the best way is the only option worth considering.

Naomi was absolutely correct. Boaz did not rest until Ruth's and Naomi's needs were met. He was prepared to act immediately on their behalf, but there was one man who was a closer relative than he. With town leaders as his witnesses, Boaz approached this nearer relative, making him aware of the losses Naomi and Ruth had suffered and their need of a kinsman redeemer. Although the other man was eager to purchase their land, he withdrew his offer when he realized that his responsibilities would also include marrying Ruth, the Moabitess. Boaz eagerly and honorably stepped in to take that man's place. He considered it his privilege to serve Naomi and Ruth as their kinsman redeemer, and to take Ruth as his wife!

Boaz is a wonderful picture of our own Savior and Redeemer, who did not rest until He had secured our redemption. Although CHRIST's love and salvation for us was not and never will be based on any remarkable qualities in us, we can certainly follow Ruth's example of displaying GODly character and unwavering faith in Him.

Our Savior will be just as honored as Boaz, and more so, when we display confidence in His ability to meet our needs. Although we are never required to "clean ourselves up" before approaching Him, we can find courage as Ruth did, to risk anything, even our perceived reputation in the eyes of others, to pursue a private audience with the Savior, to boldly sit at His feet and ask for His deliverance! We can heed Naomi's advice to "be patient," trusting that He will not rest until He has settled any matter of concern on our hearts.

The LORD's work in individual lives speaks for itself and His plans unfold at just the right time, in just the right way! Daring to embrace the hope dancing in Ruth's eyes, Naomi's arms were filled again with a baby boy to nurse. Boaz and Ruth's son, Obed, would eventually become the grandfather of King David.

A young life to rejoice in! And the new task of teaching him about the one true GOD. Despite the emptiness that threatened to bury her, Naomi had come to know the redeeming love of GOD. Now with her own faith bolstered, her heart renewed, and her true name reclaimed, she could help her grandson learn about the GOD who makes all things new again!

The living GOD heard the cries of their hearts. He used the ache of deep loss to draw Naomi and Ruth to Himself. He honored their faith in Him, whether fresh and courageous, like Ruth's, or weary and fumbling, like Naomi's. He held their longings and led them unmistakably to His exact and eternal plans for them.

Praise the Lord who has not left you without a redeemer... He will renew your life and sustain you!

Ruth 4:14-15 (NIV)

Lord, You are my portion and my cup of blessing; You hold my future.

Psalm 16:5 (CSB)

⟫ . ⟪

An inexplicable nudge lurched Martha into motion. She decided not to wait for JESUS any longer and rushed to meet Him in the road. She skipped the usual greetings and pleasantries and blurted out the swirlings in her chest. He didn't stop her. He knew that her heart was heavy and the wrestling had been fierce.

This was the Martha, who previously placed a one-on-one conversation with the Savior second to "necessary" tasks. But now, in her desperate need, it was the only thing on her mind. She was never afraid to ask the hard questions. But on this day, there were no questions, just raw outpouring of her heart. Her insistence that His presence could have made a difference, but it seemed too late. Her brother Lazarus was already dead. Four days ago, dead!

She scrambled for hope to hold onto and trust glimmered in the confidence that the resurrection was a reality she looked forward to. Her brother would one day live again! But Martha also dared to stretch beyond what she could see and know. She looked to JESUS and said, "even now, whatever You ask, the Father will give You."[24] She couldn't imagine what that might be, could she even dare to hope?

Although clearly on His way to Mary and Martha with His own purposes in mind, JESUS let time stand still to meet Martha where she was, emotionally and spiritually. To have this one-on-one conversation that was long overdue. He challenged her thinking and realigned her hope:

The truth of resurrection is not a theology or an idea,
but a Person.
Eternal life is not an eventual gift,
but a reality that includes today.
More than any reunion of a treasured earthly tie,
He wanted her to cling to *Him*.
He wanted her to understand that anything or anyone of true eternal value was never lost when safe in the Father's care.

Mary heard that JESUS was nearby and rushed out to meet Him. He could see she was broken with grief. He knew that these two sisters were very different, and He came along side each one uniquely and intimately.

JESUS didn't linger over conversation with Mary. Although she had treasured many one-on-one dialogues with Him, He knew there were no words for the sorrow that engulfed her. He simply asked, "where have you put him?"[25]

He did not explain or discuss or correct. JESUS simply chose to be present. He knew He was about to make all things new again, but He effectively said:

Let Me just be in this place with you right now.
Let Me come close to you in this time of mourning.
Let Me grieve with you.

And then, I will make it all okay again.
Then I will reveal more of Myself to you.
Then I will make all things new.
If you believe, you will see the glory of GOD!

When they reached the tomb, JESUS wept.

I can only imagine that He felt deeply the sorrow of great loss, but also His own grief about the devastating impact of sin on His creatures, whom He loved. But I wonder, too, if some of His sadness stemmed from the reality that these dear ones He had spent so much time with still failed to understand who He was, how His purposes extended far beyond the here and now, or how His sovereign power could overcome any impossibilities they might face.

Again, rather than try to explain, JESUS simply took action. He commanded that the stone be removed from the tomb where Lazarus' body was laid. Martha protested that after four days there would be a horrible stench. But JESUS gently reminded her that if she only believed, she would see the glory of GOD!

"Then JESUS raised His eyes and said, "Father, I thank You that You have heard Me. I know that You always hear Me. But because of the people standing here I said it, so that they may believe that You sent Me." When He had prayed these things, He cried out with a loud voice, "Lazarus, come forth!" The man who had died came forth, bound hand and foot with wrappings, and his face wrapped around with a cloth. JESUS said to them, "unbind him, and let him go." Then many Jews who were with Martha and Mary, and saw what JESUS had done, believed in Him."[26]

The Savior met each of these sisters uniquely and intimately in their time of grief. He chose to be present. He received their questions. He held their broken hearts. But He also knew, in that place, their hearts would be tender, open to receive a fresh glimpse of His heart, His power, and the very glory of GOD!

JESUS raised their brother Lazarus to life again. He *is* the One who makes all things new. But He also asked these sisters to do the hard thing—trust Him for His timing!

JESUS could have come sooner. He had the power to heal Lazarus and spare him from death. But He waited. Most importantly, He waited until He received clear direction from the Father that it was time to go.

Was this mysterious kindness from the Father? Would Martha and Mary, and those who stood with them, fully understand the heart and power of GOD if Lazarus had not been already dead? Four days ago, dead?! (When by their own tradition, they believed the spirit would have departed from the body.) Is it possible that the LORD delayed, even asking these dear ones to endure such depths of loss and sorrow, so that they could truly know Him? Trust Him beyond any doubt? Know that life is only, ever, always a gift from GOD? That eternal life is undeniably, exclusively within His power to grant?

I believe it is entirely possible that His kindness can feel so severe at times. But I also believe He never leaves us to wrestle through those mysterious purposes of GOD on our own. He holds our hearts, and our grief, and gently draws our hearts to see an eternal reality that transcends even our deepest losses.

ℯ . ℳ

This is our Savior. The LORD JESUS created us. He is the One who loves us so much that He gave everything to redeem us. Every moment of ours is important to Him.

He knows us intimately. And He longs for us to know Him intimately too. He will use our deep losses just to be present. To draw us to Himself. To reveal His glory!

It thrills His heart to see us run to Him. He will always meet us. He will always know exactly what we need, when we need it, and provide it abundantly.

His care is tender.
His words refocus our thinking
with eternally unchanging truth.
His power breathes life.
His presence speaks peace.

When we encounter others grieving losses big and small, we can extend the love and care of Jesus to them. We can follow His example and simply choose to be present. To listen. To grieve with them. And then, as His Spirit gives us the words, we can speak life and peace and truth that steadies them and points them back to the Savior who loves them, holds their grieving hearts and walks with them through their time of trial.

Cast your cares upon the Lord and He will sustain you. For He cares for you.

Psalm 55:22, I Peter 5:7 (NIV)

80 . 03

Read more of their stories . . . and reflect on your own!

NAOMI and RUTH
Ruth 1–4

How did each woman respond uniquely to the losses they have experienced?

They both chose the long journey to Bethlehem—what was the posture of each of their hearts as they traveled into the unknown?

How did they see themselves? How did others see them? What gives us a glimpse of how God saw them?

In what ways did the unseen yet undeniable hand of God move to provide for their needs?

What does their story reveal to us about the heart of God?

MARTHA and MARY
John 11:1–45

With what did each woman wrestle in their time of sorrow?

How did they express their pain?

How did JESUS respond uniquely to each of them in their grief?

What was additionally challenging about the timing of His visit?

Looking back, how might Mary and Martha have considered His timing to be mysterious kindness?

What did JESUS reveal about His heart through His words and actions?

What did He most want these sisters to understand more clearly?

OVERALL

What losses cast a dark shadow of grief across your heart?

How has sorrow impacted your understanding of the heart of GOD?

In what ways has the LORD met you (or gently tried to reach you) in your place of loss? How might His Presence speak peace and comfort over your pain?

What tender words from Scripture reassure your heart that He is near, holding you close when you may not "feel" His Presence?

What truth about GOD's exact and eternally purposeful plans might allow hope to rise above despair?

— • —

Who is this One we are getting to know more intimately? The LORD revealed Himself to Naomi & Ruth and to Martha & Mary as:

* the One who knows the deep ache of our losses
* the One who holds our grieving hearts, uniquely and personally
* the One who meets our longings with new hope
* the One whose care is tender
* the One whose truth refocuses our thinking
* the One whose power breathes life
* the One whose presence speaks peace
* the One who never leaves us

Chapter Seven

the One who speaks my name: blessed is she who recognizes His tender and personal care

It was the same beach. The same cove. The same rocks and ocean and sky. But it all looked different than it had one year before. The sand was littered with seaweed from a recent storm. The debris was dark, messy, tangled, smelly even. Captivated by the sun sparkling like a sea of diamonds on the water, and wooed by the lapping cadence of gentle waves, I lifted my eyes from the rubble to the horizon.

It was the first day of school and this walk on the beach had become my favorite tradition, taking a necessary pause before busy days and weeks take over. An intentional deep breath to bathe a new year in prayer, to ask for the LORD's special and unique favor over each of our kids and their teachers, and ourselves as their parents.

Just a few hours before, I sat with the kids at the breakfast table. It was so encouraging to share these words with them:

The Lord says, I will guide you along the best pathway for your life. I will advise you and watch over you. Good planning and hard work lead to success. The Lord's plans stand firm forever. His intentions can never be shaken. This work has been done with the help of our God.

Psalm 32:8, Proverbs 21:5,
Psalm 33:11, Nehemiah 6:16

That last verse really touched me since our last name, "Colaiuta," an Americanized version of an Italian name "con l'auito di Dio," means, "with the help of GOD." It felt as though He was speaking to us by name, reminding me that our kids weren't stepping into a new school year alone. He would always be with them!

I had vivid memories of that same walk one year prior. Long stretches of it were in silence, whispering quiet gratefulness for time to think and pray. As I asked the LORD for His hand upon the year ahead, I sensed an answer settling across my heart. It was not audible, but it was clear, and it was real. I distinctly remember receiving it with seriousness, but not any fear.

There will be mountains to climb this year . . .
but I will be with you every step of the way.

I stopped dead in my path. What could He possibly mean? And just as quickly as the question formed in my mind, His Spirit seemed to calm my heart and remind me that I didn't need to know the details. I could simply trust Him. For He would be with me and that was all I needed to know.

℘ . ℂℬ

She may have felt like a nobody who was invited to travel and work for a successful somebody. Then invited to be a more important somebody in that family until things didn't work out so well and she ran away, feeling again like a nobody. But there, she realized the One and only, true Somebody took notice of her and valued her enough to speak to her, comfort her, direct her, and provide for her.

Her name was Hagar. She was the Egyptian servant to Sarah, Abraham's wife. When Sarah was unable to have children, she offered Hagar to Abraham as a second wife for the purpose of being a surrogate mother, through whom Sarah might have children (a common custom of their day). When Hagar took too much pleasure in the success of her mission, Sarah treated her so harshly that Hagar ran away. Pregnant and alone in the desert, her head and heart probably swirling with a whole gamut of emotions and questions, this nobody from a pagan land encountered the one true GOD.

"Hagar, where are you coming from and where are you going?"[27] He asked. He spoke her name! Almighty GOD knew her by name and invited her to tell Him her story. She might have been surprised, but we don't read that she was afraid. She wasn't defiant. Hagar answered the LORD honestly, "I am running away from my mistress Sarah."[28]

I wonder if the years in Abraham's household helped her to learn about GOD. She might have been haughty toward Sarah, but she seemed humble before the LORD and comfortable enough to respond to Him.

GOD's words were not easy for her to hear. He directed her to return to that difficult situation and submit to her mistress.

But He also comforted her, reassuring her that He knew of her suffering, that she would have a son, and that He would multiply her offspring. He even gave her rare insight into the kind of man her son would become.

Again, we don't read that Hagar balked at the LORD's direction to her. She didn't plead her case or argue that returning to Sarah might not be the best thing to do. On the contrary, she seemed genuinely touched that GOD saw her, spoke to her and cared about her current and future well-being. She said, "You are the GOD who sees me. Truly here I have seen Him who looks after me."[29]

This nobody from a pagan land felt known, valued, and directed by Almighty GOD. We aren't told all of Hagar's thoughts, but we do know that she obeyed GOD. She returned to Sarah and bore Abraham a son, Ishmael.

What a beautiful lesson in this little part of Hagar's story. She was not the first and would not be the last to find herself in a sticky situation, with complex human relationships. GOD called her to do a hard thing—to submit to an authority who was mistreating her with unreasonable cruelty. GOD called her to trust Him and obey Him anyway.

I want to believe it was her appreciation for GOD and His provision and care for her that enabled her to obey. She was honoring Him first and He honored her by giving her the courage to do that hard thing. We don't read about Sarah treating her harshly after her return. Could it be that Hagar's humility and submission earned Sarah's respect in return? We don't know for sure. But I do believe this is a picture of a soft heart bringing about a much more positive outcome than a hard one.

May I learn from Hagar to soften my heart toward GOD first, trusting Him to care for me and meet my needs. The reassurance of His full embrace and the ability to rest in His abundant provisions can be so freeing, allowing and enabling me to open my heart to others, paving the way to enjoy healthier and more peaceful relationships!

In time, GOD fulfilled His promise to Abraham and Sarah, enabling Sarah to conceive and bear their son Isaac. For the first time in thirteen years, there was unrest within their household again. Conflict between the two half-brothers stirred up old hard feelings from Sarah. She demanded that Hagar and Ishmael be removed from the home where she would raise her own son. Upon GOD's confirmation and direction, Abraham made provisions for their journey and sent Hagar and Ishmael away.

This time, Hagar hadn't run away in fear and uncertainty, she had been sent away, definitively. Her own old hard feelings surfaced again, and those haunting voices that she was a nobody. Still. Once again, she was alone in the desert, in despair, with swirling emotions and questions. Only this time she had a young son to consider as well. Convinced that they would die of thirst, she left Ishmael in the little bit of shade she could find and separated from him because she couldn't bear to see him suffer.

In that dark place, Hagar encountered GOD for the second time. "What troubles you, Hagar? Don't be afraid. I have heard your son's voice. Go to him and take him by the hand, for I will make him into a great nation."[30]

Again, the one true GOD spoke her name! Again, He comforted her, directed her, and provided for her and her son by leading them to a spring of water. GOD was not only with her, looking after her, but He was with her son. GOD heard her son's voice crying out to Him. He heard her cries of desperation. He saw her helpless situation. And He had the answers. The one true GOD was willing and able to meet her every need. He had a plan for her life and revealed what she needed to confidently take the next step.

What confidence this gives us too. It is so comforting to know that when we run out of resources, He is right there. It is so wonderful that His provisions are perfect and not limited by events, conditions, or human relationships!

We may be different from Hagar in time and place,

circumstances and even personality, yet the LORD sees each one of us and meets us exactly where we are. He is the same GOD today! He sees and knows us and will come close to us in whatever situation we find ourselves. He calls us by name and reminds us that we are never alone and never out of options. He is always the best and only perfect option!

You are God who sees me... truly here I have seen Him who looks after me.

Genesis 16:13 (ESV)

ॐ . ৫৪

Mountains to climb? I took a deep breath. Knowing the LORD promised to be with me for every step of that climb held my heart from fear. I was truly grateful for His gentle words of preparation and prayed for the ability to trust the future to His care, without knowing what would come next.

In the year that followed, I quickly realized that mountains are beautiful from a distance, or from the top, but rarely in the middle of the climb. The narrow focus of the climb began to cave in too close, too steep.

It all seemed too big. Overwhelming. Unbelievable. Completely out of our control. I watched helplessly as the incomprehensible demands of my husband's job took an increasingly serious toll on him. They had compounded year after year, and now reached a fever pitch. Physically. Mentally. Emotionally. Spiritually.

Long hours. Ceaseless demands. Unreasonable expectations. It all seemed so unfair. Even when he finally arrived home, he was barely "present." My heart broke for the suffering he endured. Exhaustion. Defeat. Discouragement. Migraines. Inability to sleep. Occipital neuralgia. Lock jaw.

Mistreatment and injustice can be the most difficult challenges to bear. Yet the LORD seemed to be asking the hard thing—to *stay*, to persevere, to simply remain faithful to the job He had provided.

"How long, LORD? How much? What exactly are you asking of him? How do we navigate this impossible situation?" I cried out to the LORD! I pleaded with Him day after day. For the first time in my life I knew what it was to fall before Him, in full body prostration. My nose imprinted in our bedroom carpet!

It all seemed too big. The weight of this trial. So long, so hard, the right path forward so unclear. It *was* too big for us, but not too big for Him. Were we crazy to hope that we could be on the verge of something life-changing? Something that would be unbelievably hard to go through, but could lead us to a place on the other side that was better than we could have ever dreamed? Was the LORD allowing all this because He loved us too much to leave us floundering in waves of pressure He never called us to? Drowning in waves of empty expectations and goals from whom? To whom exactly was my husband giving his best?

Could there be a rescue we never saw coming? Could the doors of heaven open to pour out what we couldn't even hold?

When I didn't know what to pray, I asked the Holy Spirit to give me words.

"LORD, into Your hands I commend... (deposit, entrust, release)," I started to pray. I struggled to finish my own sentence. Was this a place of huge surrender? What did I commend to Him? My husband, our family, our home, our goals, our hopes, our priorities that seemed lost in the demands of a corporate world?

One verse steadied me:

They cried out to the Lord and He rescued them...

Psalm 107:6, 13, 19, 28 (CSB)

My prayer simply shifted to this: *"Jesus looked to the Father. Father God we look to You. We need help!"*

The Lord also used a study in Romans to ground my narrative. To provide the solid foundation of truth that was immovable regardless of the incline or the obstacles. In each new challenge, the breath of HOPE came through loud and clear:

I see you.
I love you.
I have a plan.
I will not leave you drowning in the wake of sin's destruction,
in you or around you.
Trust My love, even when it seems severe,
knowing it is kindness drawing your heart to Mine.
Reach for My rescue, as often as you need it,
knowing it is sufficient and eternally secure.
Reach for Me. Ask Me to help you.
Find that I am here.
Always.

His truth steadied me. But the onslaught continued. Just when we thought my husband's long hard trial could not possibly get any worse, it did. Unthinkably. Another blow. How could he continue to submit to such authority? Work hard with integrity that was utterly disregarded? But no other path seemed available.

He was weary. Horribly disheartened. He looked to the Lord for the strength to face each new day. Somehow, he recovered each night and stepped bravely back into work each morning.

I continued to helplessly watch. And pray.

℘ . ℭ

*You don't know what I am doing
right now, but one day you will.*

John 13:7 (NLT, paraphrase)

In many challenging times over many years, I have "stumbled" across this verse just when I needed reminding that Almighty GOD sees and knows a much bigger picture than I will ever understand.

I found myself right back there. Again.

I was waiting. I was praying. I had longings. My heart was heavy with burdens for this man I loved, struggling so severely!

My mind raced ahead and I thought I was so clever to come up with some really wonderful solutions. But He said, *"be still."*

Again, we had deep soul wrestling, my LORD and I. He was so gracious to receive my rants, my tears, my questions, my premature excitement about the latest, greatest plan I dreamt up. And He faithfully asked me again and again, *"are you willing to just trust Me?"*

In that place of grappling which were nudges from Him and which were impatient, flesh-fueled impulses to fix and resolve, and in that season of great uncertainty and mounting questions with few answers, I opened John 13.

It is a well-known passage where the LORD JESUS stooped to wash His disciples' feet.

Tucked away in an upper room together, JESUS' closest followers were enjoying final hours with Him before He would fulfill the Father's plan of redemption and ultimately leave them to return to the Father's side as their risen, glorified LORD.

JESUS poured into His disciples that night, teaching them as much as they were able to receive. But in the tender moments recorded in John 13, He paused those spoken lessons simply to serve them, to teach them how to care for one another as He cared for each of them.

They called Him Master and Teacher, yet He girded Himself with a towel and knelt to wash their feet. One by one, He took their feet in His hands and washed away the dirt and debris from the dusty roads. His actions enabled them to experience His personal care and feel His touch, to meet His gaze and exchange thoughts without words. Thoughts meant intimately for each of them, directly from His heart. They had worked hard by His side, ministering to others, watching His steps and following close behind. Now He stooped to renew and refresh them, individually and personally.

The LORD JESUS came to Peter, who could barely contain himself. "No, LORD! Why are You doing this?!" he protested. It seemed as if Peter had his own grand ideas and was outraged that the One he knew to be the true Messiah should take on such a task. I wonder if he even felt honorable in refusing to let this scene continue. In his own judgment of the situation, he missed the beauty of those intimate encounters.

And right there in the middle of the passage, where I had completely forgotten it originated, were those exact same words I had pondered so often, "You don't know what I am doing now, but one day you will."[31] Yes, much as I have always thought, the LORD JESUS was thinking and acting upon a much bigger picture than Peter could realize. But finding those words in the middle of this scene shifted my perspective!

A new train of thought began to roll across my heart…

Those heavy burdens, those severe struggles, those painful moments, those swirling questions… Those were the times when I was tempted to think the LORD was off somewhere else, busy attending to the plan I couldn't see just yet, and asking for me to trust that He would circle back at just the right time to fill me in.

But seeing these words in the setting of John 13, I heard His gentle voice flipping the script. Could the Holy Spirit have been tuning my heart to see that it was in those times that the LORD JESUS was coming closer than ever, to tenderly and intimately care for me? For my husband? That He was removing dirt and debris, renewing and refreshing, and preparing us for the next part of our journey?

When the days and weeks seemed long and hard, could I tuck further away with Him to let Him touch me, cleanse me, teach me, and ask me again to simply trust Him?

Could I trust the work He was doing in my husband's heart in the depths of his own struggles? Was I willing to understand that what He was accomplishing through his own wrestling was truly precious and tender and intimate between him and the Savior? A tremendous gift from GOD that I would never want him to miss?

Did I believe the LORD was big enough, strong enough and tender enough to walk us through any and every circumstance, joyous or painful? Was I willing to rest, really rest in the knowing that His Father's plan was our Father's plan too? That it was exactly purposeful and right on time, but that He never asked us to do the waiting alone? Could I look for the ways that He stooped to serve and care for us, especially when I couldn't possibly understand what He was doing?

There would still be many steps along the way that wouldn't make sense to me, that would be difficult, confusing, painful, grueling even. But it was all part of the journey that drew me ever closer to the Savior. In step with Him, just as He aligned with the Father's plans.

At any cost, the LORD JESUS trusted the Father. He obeyed. He rejoiced to see the plan completed. And so would we.

I couldn't imagine how, but I felt bold faith strengthening. I proclaimed with surprising confidence that one day it would all make sense. One day the current struggles would be past. One day the tears would flow as we saw with clearer vision exactly what He had been working on all along. One day we would acknowledge the grace with which He had welcomed us to have a part in fulfilling the Father's plan—right beside Him!

I professed with Job, "yet will I trust Him."[32]

The Lord encircles us, instructs us, keeps us as the apple of His eye... as an eagle stirs up its nest, hovers over its young, spreading out its wings, taking them up, carrying them on its wings, so the Lord alone leads us.

Deuteronomy 32:10-12 (NKJV)

℧ . ℭ

The night stretched long after a painfully quiet Sabbath. The stillness made the events of the previous day pound on repeat through her heart. It is very likely she didn't sleep all night. By early morning, still before any light of day, she just couldn't bear it any longer. She got up, got dressed and went to the only place she really wanted to be. The last place she had seen her Savior. Laid in a new tomb.

When she got there, the stone had been rolled away and even in the darkness, she could see that the tomb was empty! A surge of panic and fear shot through her. She ran to Peter and John to tell them that His body had been moved, and she anxiously looked to them for help to find Him. They ran back to the tomb ahead of her and found just what she had discovered—an empty tomb. Just as perplexed but beginning to believe what JESUS had told them about His death and resurrection, Peter and John returned home. She was alone again but couldn't leave.

She stooped to look in the tomb again and this time it was filled with light! Two angels sat where JESUS' body had been. They asked why she was weeping. "Because they have taken away my LORD, and I do not know where they have laid Him."[33]

She hadn't missed a single step of her LORD's journey. She had traveled with Him, cared for His needs. She had been close enough to hear His final words from the cross, to see Him take His last breath, and to watch as Joseph and Nicodemus prepared His body and laid Him in that new tomb. She just wanted to be near Him. She always took notice of where He was and did everything she could to be close to Him. Now she couldn't find Him, and she was heartbroken.

For some reason, before hearing the angels' response, she turned and noticed a man standing behind her. In the early morning light and through her tears, she couldn't make out His features and assumed He was the gardener. "Please, if you have taken away my LORD, please tell me where He is and I will go and get Him."[34]

"Mary."[35]

She heard Him say her name and immediately she knew it was her Savior! Only *His* voice could sound like that. Only *His* heart could communicate so much by just speaking her name. Grief had clouded her vision, but she recognized His voice speaking to her! She was too overjoyed to worry about the how or the why, she simply fell at His feet.

We don't know much about Mary Magdalene, only that JESUS had cast seven demons out of her and from that time, she rarely left His side. She was eternally delivered and impacted by JESUS and she overflowed with love and devotion to Him. She just wanted to be near Him. She sought Him out. Even when He died, she took careful notice of where His body was laid and went to the tomb to be as close to Him as she could be. When she saw Him again, she fell at His feet and clung to Him as if she would never let go. JESUS gently but firmly redirected her, "I have not yet ascended to My Father. Go, tell My brothers that I am ascending to My Father and your Father, to My GOD and your GOD!"[36]

It seems that every choice Mary made may have been through a few key filters:

Does it get me closer to JESUS?

Does it keep me near Him?

Does it help me know Him better,

recognize His voice more clearly?

How else can I serve Him?

There is no one like JESUS! I can't get enough of Him. Ever!

Passion for her Savior led Mary to the tomb that morning. He was her first and only priority! And He met her there. He gave her a precious gift. She was the first person to see the Risen Savior. He spoke her name! He touched her heart. He was slowly helping her understand that although He would be ascending to the Father, His Spirit would still be with her. She would no longer need to cling to His physical body. As her LORD, He gave her what might have been her very first assignment, to "go and tell." He was gently leading her away from paralyzing grief to new joy that would fuel her service for Him!

Mary's encounter with JESUS on Resurrection Sunday touches me deeply. I am reminded again that our Savior is so incredibly personal. His interactions with us communicate volumes in a word. He knows us individually and meets us exactly where we are to reassure our hearts and lead us to the next step in loving and serving Him well.

Mary's devotion to the LORD challenges my heart. How often do I put my own decisions through her filters? Really it comes down to this: how much can I say "no" to so I can spend more time with Him, so I can seek His face? To hear His voice more clearly, to get to know Him better? What a tender and precious train of thought—not to brow beat me away from less desirable choices, but simply to draw me to the better choice every time. Closer to my Savior. Nearer, still nearer to JESUS!

The Lord is close to the brokenhearted
and saves those whose spirits are crushed.

Psalm 34:18

℘ . ℂ

As I reflected on the year that had passed since that first prayer walk on the beach, I could only give praise to the One who had been faithful to those words.

There will be mountains to climb this year,
but I will be with you every step of the way.

He prepared my heart so that when struggles came, I could find a rock-solid place to stand, on His promises. As I walked along that same beach and had the chance to look back over twelve months, I could see more clearly how He had drawn closer than ever to personally walk us through each trial with tenderness and care! I felt a surge of new confidence that any days ahead would be the same.

I offered thanksgiving for the LORD's faithfulness over the previous year and His promises given that very morning with which to step bravely into the new one.

I wondered if He had anything new to reveal to my heart? What banner might He want me to stretch over this new season? These are the thoughts that came...

Slow down.
Be still.
Treasure what is right in front of you
without rushing past.

Your kids are growing older, both in high school now.
Your time with them is fleeting. It's ok to let go
more than ever before and leave space
for Me to work in their hearts.
Trust Me with the trials, some of which
are still ongoing from last year,
some will be new challenges ahead.
Embrace where I have placed you.
In love and faithfulness, simply seek My face
and love and serve your family.

My mind drifted back to our verses at the breakfast table and a sacrifice of praise spilled freely from my heart:

You are the One who watches over us. You are the One who speaks our names and lifts our heads, who draws our eyes from the dark, messy, tangled debris of any recent storm to the horizon and to HOPE rising, fresh each day with the sun, and it is dazzling! You are the One who guides us, who blesses good planning and hard work with success. Your plans are never shaken. Your help is what sees us to any finish line. We can only offer praise and thanksgiving from deeply grateful hearts!

The Lord is my strength and shield.
I trust in Him with all my heart.
He helps me and my heart is filled
with joy. I burst out in songs of
thanksgiving. The Lord gives His

*people strength. He is a safe
fortress for His anointed. The Lord
blesses His people with peace.*

Psalm 28:7–8, 29:11

℘ . ℅

Read more of their stories . . . and reflect on your own!

HAGAR
Genesis 16, 21

In what situation did Hagar encounter GOD?

What do we learn about the heart of GOD in reaching out to her?

How did she respond to Him?

What did Hagar learn about GOD?

What options did Hagar have in her challenging situation?

How did she know which next step to take?

MARY MAGDALENE
Luke 8:1–3, Mark 15:37–47, John 20:1–18

What drew Mary to the tomb after JESUS' death?

What was heavy on her heart?

How did JESUS reveal Himself to her?

How did He realign her thinking? What new job did He give her to do?

OVERALL

What times of suffering have left you battle-weary, heart-broken, defeated?

In what ways has the LORD come close to care for you? To speak truth that realigns your thinking? That gives you hope?

How has He been tuning your heart to recognize His voice? To know He calls to you by name? To receive fresh direction from a Savior who loves you?

∞ . ∞

Who is this One we are getting to know more intimately? The LORD revealed Himself to Hagar and Mary Magdalene as:

* the One who welcomes dialogue with us
* the One who knows us by name
* the One who asks us to do hard things
* the One who gives us strength and courage to obey
* the One who hears and answers our cries
* the One who gives us new insight
* the One who is able to meet our needs, miraculously and abundantly
* the One who directs us to the best next step

Chapter Eight

the One who is worthy of my surrender: blessed is she who is broken and spilled out

"Hey, sorry if this comes out of nowhere. Is there a time one day soon when we could talk privately? I need a safe place to unburden a deep weight on my heart."

I t had all gotten bigger than big. I was crumbling under the weight of my husband's long, hard trial. I literally kept notes of physical symptoms I witnessed as his body struggled to manage the stress. I lived with very present fear that he would collapse, and I would need to call 911.

It seemed endless, and grueling. With each passing day, terror gripped my chest. My muscles were tense, my eyes were weary from fighting back tears of concern and frustration. My closet doors were covered with written prayers and thoughts and verses from time spent in my own little war room! I felt the LORD was asking me to learn the rhythm of trusting Him while circumstances remained unchanged.

In my most private moments, pouring my heart out to Him, a growing question terrified me. Was He trying to prepare me to lose my husband? Even the thought of such an incomprehensible loss engulfed me. It hung like a heavy cloud, stunning me into silent stillness. It was unthinkable, yet unavoidable.

For months, I didn't dare breathe a word of those fears to anyone. I was sure no one would understand how real that possibility seemed to me. But it was more than I could hold on my own. I needed help!

The LORD sent me "ground angels."

A very few, prayerfully chosen friends, like the one who received my text that day, sat with me in coffee shops, on park benches or their own sofas while I sobbed my way through my story. Unburdening my deepest, darkest fears. They held my hand and prayed for me when I couldn't speak the words. They welcomed SOS texts any time of the day or night and sent back Spirit-led prayers with His Words to comfort, steady, and direct my heart.

I knew it was not easy for them to receive and process all I shared with them. I treasured the precious gift of their unwavering friendship. I believed those tender exchanges were the hallowed ground where testimony of GOD's grace and power could be rooted until the rest of the story could unfold.

Heart to heart, those dear friends reminded me to trust the LORD to work in my husband's heart. That He was asking me to leave space for that work to happen. But to allow my husband to watch me sink into the Father, finding my steady place in Him. To continue to pray for the vision to see the Father's plan, and for the courage to follow.

I asked the LORD for help. His strength to walk me through whatever turn of events each new day might bring. To keep my eyes fixed. Not paralyzed by fear of loss but directed moment by moment by the Father. His answer week after week was simple, but direct, *"Just love him. Treasure what is right in front of you for as long as you are given that gift to hold."*

My best and only option was to entrust my husband, and the length of his days, to the One who writes his story as well as mine.

I looked for any opportunity to tenderly care for him, support him, and savor our times together. (It is a level of intentionality that stays with me still and sweetens the continuing growth of our marriage!)

One memorable morning, a new thought settled over my heart. I remember the exact spot, standing in my bathroom, getting ready to step bravely into another day. The LORD brought a picture of Abraham and Isaac to mind. He seemed to say to me:

"I've been testing you. I needed to know I had your whole heart. I needed you to know you could trust Me. With anything. Even with this man I have given to walk beside you. As sorrow gripped you, you turned to Me. You didn't plead with Me to keep him on earth. You simply asked Me for the strength to walk whatever path lay ahead in a way that honored Me."

In that moment, the heaviness I had been carrying lifted. I could not say that the LORD promised He would not call my husband Home to heaven ahead of me. But I felt, for the time being, that He had given back to me what I had willingly surrendered to Him. My earthly partner. I wept in waves of gratefulness.

ⅎ . ℻

After months of earnest prayer, my husband braved the vast world of online job postings. He updated a resume he hadn't looked at in close to a decade and began the arduous task of submitting applications for a new position. He said it was humbling and vulnerable to put himself out there again. He didn't honestly know where to begin, but we trusted the LORD to direct us to the right options. For the first time in years, we prayed together that the LORD would show us a new path forward!

An exciting opportunity quickly materialized! Seemingly

overnight, the interview process rolled forward with quickening speed. Alarmed but excited, I was swept away in the anticipation of what could be, searching available homes and schools in a location we dearly longed to live. The Virginia mountains!

The northern hills, a short drive from our favorite vacation home for the past twenty years, a few short hours from our childhood homes and favorite Christian summer camp. I was overwhelmed with emotion, just imagining that the LORD's plans could place us where we didn't ever allow ourselves to dream of living. It all seemed to be falling miraculously into place.

Until it didn't.

My husband was not chosen for the job. The door was closed. Slammed shut.

Somehow, he'd sensed this inevitable outcome. He was inexplicably at peace that it just wasn't the right place for us. Lost in my own dream world, it took me by surprise, and I crumbled into a puddle of tears on the floor. It wasn't pretty. I had to face the strength of my own longings, the growing homesickness I had managed to stuff down year after year. It all broke open in the rawest sense.

I cried myself to sleep that night, asking the LORD to hold me until I could see things more clearly. My sweet husband held me too and reassured me that he truly believed the LORD closed that door because He had something better in mind. That He was using this long, complicated trial to get our attention and help us hunger only for His best.

Fresh strength dawned with a new day and I wrote these words to our praying friends:

"I can only say this: "yet will I trust Him." I know our GOD is trustworthy and His plans are right and good and right on time. I know He loves us like crazy. I know His tender hands are the ones that will hold my heart and tune it to His. Again. And I know that His Spirit is the one who will prompt my heart to offer Him praise in the midst of the

heartache. To hold out my longings in willing surrender all over again, trusting Him to help me settle in where He has placed us and get busy doing the work He has for us here. I don't doubt that the blessings He showers us with daily in this place will bring great comfort and gratitude! THANK YOU again for walking this path with us. We treasure you and your prayers!"

ℴ . ℴ

The job search continued. Countless applications, questionnaires, phone screenings. We felt jostled and battered as several more possibilities seemed promising, only to see them fall dead in the water as the door slammed shut, again. Harrisburg. Kansas City. Louisville. Greensboro. Our hearts seemed in agreement that a move closer to home and to family was the right one. But the answer continued to be NO. Gentle but firm. NO.

Those NO answers awakened an old ache. That long string of beads that seemed to spell only one thing. L O S S. And now S U F F E R I N G. And not just mine, but my husband's. How much longer could he endure? It was hard to keep believing the LORD had a plan. That His plan was good. That His answer *was* coming.

One morning, I sensed the nudge to set my normal devotions aside and sit with an empty note open on my phone. To let all other voices fall silent and simply ask the LORD, *"what do You want me to hear from You today?"*

The nudge felt "outside of me," so I sat up to take notice and worked hard to still my body and mind to really listen. I *needed* to hear from Him! Those mountains we had been climbing seemed steeper than ever. Questions raged, cries for rescue from my prayer closet became more desperate and answers seemed increasingly illusive!

O our God, we don't know what to do,
but our eyes are on You!

2 Chronicles 20:12 (ESV)

We needed help! What would He reveal that might answer the deep pleading to understand His plan?

This is what fell across my heart: *"You are loved. Don't ever doubt that."*

It was so simple, yet so profound. He knew in those dark days when His answers seemed silent, this would be my most dangerous temptation—to doubt His love for us.

His words to my heart were so tender, and so very deeply touching! My whole body softened, my eyes welled up, and the burning questions I thought might be answered in that moment all melted away.

Almighty GOD, Creator of heaven and earth, not only saw us, and cared for us, He LOVED us! With a love like no other! He is sovereign. He can be trusted. Although the path forward might remain a mystery, I could rest in knowing that He would always be with us. He would lead us to the right path. He would see us safely to the other side of this valley.

You are very precious to God! ... see
how very much the Father loves us!

Daniel 10:19, I John 3:1

ॐ . ☪

Hannah's heart was broken. She was so distraught that she couldn't even eat. She stepped away from the rest of the family to find a private place to weep. Surely, she would find solace in the LORD's tabernacle.

Year after year, a deep ache overwhelmed her. With each passing trip to Shiloh, where their family offered sacrifices to the LORD with the help of the priests at the tabernacle, the road became unthinkably more painful. For the length of their marriage, Hannah had been unable to bear children for her husband, Elkanah. The taunts from his other wife, Peninnah, who had born him many children, were increasingly and unbearably cruel. Hannah fell to her knees, pouring out her anguish to the LORD.

Lord of Hosts, take notice of Your servant's affliction, remember and not forget me, and give Your servant a son.

I Samuel 1:11 (ESV)

Eli, the priest, saw her. Although he initially misjudged her tears and silent prayers as a sad impact of wine, he quickly realized her agony was genuine. She pleaded with the LORD from a sincere heart. Eli told her, "go in peace, and may the GOD of Israel grant the petition you've requested from Him."[37]

The LORD answered her prayers and entrusted to her a son. His name was Samuel.

Year after year, Hannah had brought everything to the LORD in prayer. Faithfully, consistently, with unwavering faith. No matter how she might make sense of her situation, her pain, or her longings, GOD was the One to whom she could unburden her heart. Again and again and again.

Hannah was brave enough to trust GOD with those longings. And with His answer. She voluntarily offered to give Samuel back to GOD, to serve Him in the tabernacle for the rest of his life.

Scripture tells us that she saw Samuel once a year, when their family traveled to worship the LORD at Shiloh. She displayed unbelievable courage and self-sacrifice to value the plan GOD had for his life, and to encourage him in that path.

Hannah's promise to give Samuel to the LORD might, at first glance, seem like a desperate bargaining tool. But as I spend more time pondering her story, I wonder if she understood the need in Israel for a true man of GOD and was burdened to pray that she could be part of GOD's provision! Could it be, as she noticed with growing concern the deterioration of the integrity within Eli's family of priests, that her prayer became even more earnest? "Please LORD, remember Your servant, give me a son, that I may give him to the LORD all the days of his life."

We can only guess that Hannah was a prayer warrior. Over the years of waiting for GOD to give her a son, it is very possible that she was also praying for the LORD to bless the nation of Israel with true men of GOD to serve Him. I have no doubt that her prayers continued for Samuel, growing and learning and serving the LORD far away from her. And I imagine there were tender moments along the way when she came to know the closeness of the GOD who loved her and answered her prayers. That He revealed things to her that few people around her truly understood. That He prepared her heart to willingly surrender the very answer to her prayers.

The LORD honored Hannah for her devotion to Him, and for her sacrifice. He opened her womb and blessed her with three more sons and two daughters. Hannah poured out her heart again to the LORD. This time in worship, praise and thanksgiving:

My heart rejoices in the Lord,
O, how the Lord has blessed me!

I rejoice in Your salvation...
there is no one besides You!

I Samuel 2:1-2

ଞ . ଔ

"What have you learned from this week's study about repentance?"

I pondered that Bible study question for days. During that time, the LORD led me to the same question again and again. In an online devotional message. In a song on the radio. In my own reading in my *One Year Bible*. In *Daily Light*.

Repentance. It was clear He was shining a glaring light on my heart. But it was not immediately obvious to me. From what, exactly, was He asking me to repent?

I left the question blank on my page and gathered with our sweet group of ladies to discuss the first few chapters of I Samuel.

Eli, the priest, had allowed corruption and contempt for GOD's law to run rampant in his sons. GOD's chosen nation, Israel, was paying a harsh price for abandoning His commandments and callously disregarding His covenant.

While he was still young, GOD touched the heart of Samuel, who listened and obeyed the voice of GOD. The LORD used Samuel to call GOD's people to repentance. To wholeheartedly return to GOD.

At the close of a sobering discussion about the pitfalls of sin and the consequences of allowing compromise to slowly draw our hearts away from GOD, that final question was posed. I felt the nudge to speak, to bare my soul and confess the glaring spotlight on my heart all week.

I hesitated. "*You don't need to speak it out loud. You haven't even pieced it all together yet. You're still processing,*" I told myself. But the

Spirit's prompting became unavoidable. *"No. You do need to speak it! You need these ladies to hold you accountable!"*

I blurted out the first words before fully deciding to speak. The sound of my own voice startled me and everyone's eyes fixed on my face. I knew I had to be brave and let it all come spilling out.

The full realization dawned as I formed each word:

"Twelve years ago, we said there was a stronger pull on our hearts. To follow the LORD wherever He would lead us. Even when that leading took us far from faces and places we loved and loss was real. We've said so many times that despite the heartbreak, His plan is best and we would make the same choice all over again.

I wonder... in this very moment ... if I have grown weary of that call?

Have I selfishly allowed my own longings for "home" to get tangled up in my earnest prayers for rescue for my husband? Is this the hold-out place in my heart where the LORD is calling me to repent?"

Those sweet ladies didn't speak, didn't move. They allowed the silence to hold my grief as I sobbed through the severe mercy of GOD reaching my heart.

"Maybe He knew all along that we could move "home" to the northern hills and I would still have this ache. Twelve years ago, He asked me just to trust Him. In the years since, He has been asking me to trust Him more deeply, with my husband's health and with the course He mapped out for us.

Maybe He brought me here, where I didn't really want to be, because He loves me too much to leave me broken, longing for something only He can satisfy.

Maybe He has been trying to show me all along that "home" is where He leads us. "Home" is wherever He can draw us closer to Himself. "Home" is where He is. In surrendering my definition of "home," maybe He is helping me to see that there is no sweeter "home" than the one I open for Him to fill—in my own heart."

My heart broke free that day. An enormous weight was lifted. I felt a wave of peace I couldn't describe. I told my husband, "I don't know if this has burdened you or not, but if so, I need to release you from any responsibility you feel to move me back to the northern hills. I have surrendered it to the LORD, recommitting my whole heart to the stronger pull we have answered all along. To follow Him wherever He will lead us."

> *Return to the Lord with all your heart, with weeping and mourning, rend your heart. For the Lord is gracious and compassionate, abounding in steadfast love.*

> Joel 2:12-13 (ESV)

℘ . ℭ

one day a plain village woman
driven by love for her Lord
recklessly poured out a valuable essence
disregarding the scorn

. . .

broken and spilled out
just for love of You, Jesus
my most precious treasure
lavished on Thee

Broken and Spilled Out by Steve Green, 1984

Three of the gospels in the New Testament describe this event. In John 12, this plain village woman is identified as Mary, who chose to sit at the feet of JESUS while her sister Martha worried herself about too many details.

Mary showed "reckless" abandon. She poured out her most valuable treasure. She did it out of love for her LORD.

How did she know when and how to push the other concerns aside and dive in headfirst, not looking back? She had spent time at JESUS' feet! She recognized His voice when it spoke to her heart. In that moment, nothing else mattered and she enjoyed the freedom to give everything she had as the LORD directed her. Her actions honored JESUS. They reflected an understanding of GOD's plan of redemption. Mary brought Him glory!

But she did something else. Fragrance from that ointment "filled the house!"[38] Mary's act of love, unapologetically displayed for her LORD, impacted everyone around her. It changed the atmosphere in their home. It brought the focus toward JESUS. And the aroma was sweet!

To anoint and honor the LORD JESUS, Mary broke open and spilled out a costly perfume. Valued at a years' wages. Pure spikenard was used to anoint priests and kings. When others rebuked and condemned her actions as a horrible waste, JESUS spoke in Mary's defense, recognizing her understanding of another use for spikenard. To prepare a body for burial. He had been trying to tell His disciples that He would die, in accordance with the Father's will. But few, if any of them, understood.

Mary's heart beat in tune with her Savior's, in step with the Father's plans. She courageously ignored the judgment and misunderstanding around her to honor the LORD as He anticipated His darkest hours. It is possible the LORD JESUS carried the aroma of her anointing with Him through His brutal trial, crucifixion, burial, and glorious resurrection.

Our great High Priest. Our coming King. The One who died

to conquer death once and for all. He is worthy of our sincerest worship, at any cost!

Leave her alone. She has done a beautiful thing for Me.

Mark 14:6 (NIV, ESV)

ထ . ကვ

The waiting had been long. Agonizingly long. The trial had been severe. To the very brink of what we thought capable of enduring. The LORD's strength in our weakness carried us, one weary step at a time. His Spirit drew our hearts to trust His love and reach for His rescue. So. Many. Times.

But nothing is quite as powerful as full-heart surrender.

The day after my heart broke free in that circle of sweet Bible study friends, my husband's job search took a sudden turn. A possibility he had considered "a stretch" crossed his mind months before. A work-from-home option that would allow us to live anywhere. Or stay right where we were. He had taken the brave step to pursue it, trusting the LORD's nudge to submit his resume. But there was no response. For months.

Now on the heels of full surrender, the call came.

Wheels were set in motion that day. A short time later, he was able to give his notice and shift gears into an exciting new venture! One that is more perfectly suited for him than we could imagine.

The LORD confirmed that we heard Him correctly seven years ago. This is exactly where He purposely placed us. We would be staying in south Florida for the foreseeable future.

A surrendered heart has different eyes. This home that felt "temporary" to me for seven long years suddenly appeared fresh and new, like I was exploring it for the first time! I saw the many things about our home that I truly treasure. The gifts of this community, our naturally beautiful surroundings, our church family. For the first time, I was genuinely grateful to the LORD that He called us to *stay*!

We often wondered about His purposes in our long season of waiting through the uncertainty. I believe it was the desperate hunger for His heart and the wrestling to understand His plan that positioned our hearts to receive His best with joy.

What a wonder to treasure this place where I was broken and spilled out. Where I surrendered my husband first, and finally my longings for the northern hills. Where we counted the cost, but still chose to follow the LORD. Out of trust and obedience that has always propelled us, but now also out of worship.

For He is worthy of the surrender of my whole heart.

It is His home.

૭ . ૯

Read more of their stories here...

HANNAH
I Samuel 1–2

What was the cry of Hannah's heart?

How did she respond to hurtful actions against her?

To whom did she confide her deepest longings?

How did the LORD honor her faithfulness to Him?

With what act of surrender and worship did Hannah honor the LORD in return?

How was Hannah's willing surrender a turning point in her story and that of GOD's people?

MARY OF BETHANY
John 11, 12:1–8

What was the longing of Mary's heart?

How did she respond to hurtful words against her?

What did she surrender to the LORD? In what ways did her gift honor Him?

How did JESUS honor her in return?

How did her actions change the atmosphere in their home?

OVERALL

What anguish of your heart could you pour out before the LORD?

What verses encourage you that you can trust Him with your longings?

What hold-out places in your heart might the LORD be calling you to surrender?

How might it touch His heart to receive your most treasured gift?

ᘓ . ᘔ

Who is this One we are getting to know more intimately? The LORD revealed Himself to Hannah and Mary of Bethany as:

* the One whose love is sure and steadfast (even when we are tempted to doubt it)
* the One who sees us and values us
* the One who hears our prayers
* the One who can be trusted with our longings and our deepest fears
* the One who is worthy of our worship
* the One who captivates our singular focus
* the One who treasures the surrender of our whole heart to Him

Chapter Nine

the One who wins my heart: blessed is she who believes He is precious

"This is not the day I gave you life, this is just the day I introduced you to the world and placed you in a family. Angels rejoiced in this day. All of heaven still rejoices as you seek to delight the Father's heart by delighting in His Son."

These sweet thoughts drifted across my heart as I opened my eyes on my birthday. I thanked the LORD for another milestone and asked Him to show me His desires for the year to come. I jotted down the thoughts that came:

"Desire to know Me.
Experience the depth of My love.
See others with My eyes and My heart.
And love them as I have loved you."

The whole morning felt like an outpouring of the LORD's abundant gifts to me. The words from my *One Year Bible* seemed to sum up months of being held together by His unfailing love:

I will boast only in the Lord. Let all who are helpless take heart. Come, let us tell of the Lord's greatness, let us exalt His Name together! I prayed to the Lord and He answered me. He freed me from all my fears. Those who look to Him for help will be radiant with joy; no shadow of shame will darken their faces. Taste and see that the Lord is good! Oh, the joys of those who take refuge in Him! Fear the Lord ... those who fear Him will have all they need. Those who trust in the Lord will lack no good thing.

Psalm 34:2–5, 8–10

I felt the nudge to turn on Pandora to bathe the day with Contemporary Christian Praise music. Every single song for two hours touched my heart and showered me with GOD's truth and tender love. My very own, Divinely designed play list! I scrambled to write down as many song titles as I could and took the time to download every single one of them into my phone. It was a surprise birthday gift I will never forget.

My husband was traveling, in preparation for his new job. With eager anticipation I looked forward to seeing him later that day. Our Savior had rescued us. He stepped in to do for us what we were incapable of doing for ourselves. He was using my birthday to flood my heart with reminders of His faithful love and care. Reminders that we were fully known and fully loved—by Him. This is the One who had won our hearts, had carried us through the unthinkable and set our feet on solid ground. I couldn't wait to see my husband walk through the door, so we could share the joy of that day together.

ℴ . ℭ

It was an ordinary day that became rather extraordinary. Rebekah grabbed her pot and went to the spring to draw water for their household. As she turned back toward home, a stranger approached her, asking for water.

She couldn't quite explain what compelled her to show the man such kindness, but she graciously offered him a drink and returned to the spring countless more times to collect enough water to supply his camels as well.

The man thanked her and presented her with gifts. A gold nose ring and two gold bracelets. He asked about her family and if there was room in her father's house for his company to spend the night.

She still couldn't explain why she felt comfortable enough to respond to his questions, but freely shared that she was the daughter of Bethuel, the son that Milcah bore to Nahor. She also encouraged him to bring his men and their camels to spend the night at their house.

Rebekah was surprised to learn that this man was the chief servant of her uncle, Abraham. He bowed low to worship the LORD and praised Him for prospering his journey. The GOD of his master Abraham had faithfully led him to their extended family.

When all were gathered for the evening meal, the man refused to eat until he had told his true intentions. Their curiosity was piqued! What could be so important that he wouldn't even eat before explaining his purpose?

First, there was news that GOD had blessed their relative, Abraham, abundantly. And then, to everyone's surprise, they learned that in their old age, GOD had given Abraham and Sarah a son! Isaac was now a man and Abraham strictly instructed his servant to travel back to his family to find him a wife. Abraham trusted the LORD to lead his servant to the girl He had chosen for Isaac.

The man shared amazing details about his prayers to the LORD as he approached the spring earlier that day. Knowing no one, He asked GOD to make it clear by her actions which girl was the one He had chosen. In every detail, Rebekah was the answer to his prayers—specifically offering him water to drink and sufficient water for this camels as well. He boldly asked if Rebekah's family would give their blessing for her to return with him to be Isaac's wife.

Her father and brother wholeheartedly agreed, "this is from the LORD! Take Rebekah and let her become the wife of your master's son, as the LORD has directed."[39] The man again worshiped the LORD and brought out more gifts for Rebekah. Gold and silver jewelry and articles of clothing. She was showered with abundance from a man who loved her before he even met her!

The whole family rejoiced over their meal that night. When morning arrived, Abraham's servant was anxious to return to his master and his son, Isaac. Rebekah's family protested that it was all happening too quickly. They asked if she could stay with them for ten more days before departing. But the man was determined to return to his master without delay.

Her father and brother asked Rebekah, "will you go with this man?" She simply said, "I will go."[40] Provisions were gathered. The camels made ready. Rebekah's family spoke a blessing over her. And they departed.

It was a long journey to meet Isaac. But with each passing step, Rebekah's heart beat faster. She longed to see his face, to know him fully. She kept her eyes on the horizon, watching for him.

And then, at last she could see him in the distance! He came out to meet her, took her by the hand and led her to their new home. Rebekah was a great comfort to Isaac after his mother Sarah's death and Scripture tells us he loved her.

What gave Rebekah the courage to travel with a stranger to a foreign land, to become the wife of a man she had never met? She acknowledged the hand of GOD. The LORD had been preparing her heart to leave her former life and follow without fully knowing the new path to which He pointed. There were no video tours or online photos to search to bolster her confidence, but she had heard enough about this son, Isaac, and his father, Abraham, and their abundant riches freely offered to her, to win her heart.

Through the testimony of a foreign man clearly touched by the reality of the one true GOD, the LORD's perfect plan was unmistakable. Rebekah placed her faith in the truth that was spoken to her. She joyfully received the gracious gifts freely extended to her. And her heart simply replied, "Yes."

"Who is that man coming to meet us?"
"It is my master's son."
She became his wife, and he loved her.

Genesis 24:65, 67

80 . 03

Rebekah's story is mine as well. I join with all who trust the LORD JESUS as our Savior, believing He is precious! I have seen the hand of GOD, felt His Spirit move.

The LORD has been preparing my heart to leave my former life, confined by a "pretty little box" of my own making and simply follow without fully knowing any new path to which

He points. There are no video tours or online photos to search to bolster my confidence about the Home He is preparing for me. But I have heard enough about this Son, JESUS, and His Father, and their abundant riches freely offered to me, to win my heart.

I now have the opportunity to offer my own testimony of the one true GOD who has made Himself real to me. So many times and in so many glorious ways! May my words of witness help others to trace His perfect plan, unmistakably.

I am on a long journey to meet my Savior. With each passing step, my heart beats faster. I long to see His face, to know Him fully. I fix my eyes on the horizon, eagerly watching for Him.

And then, at last I will see Him! The LORD JESUS will come to meet me, take me by the hand and lead me Home. I will worship Him with my whole heart and celebrate with joy overflowing, basking in His extravagant love for me.

I am my Beloved's and my Beloved is mine. His banner over me is love.

Song of Songs 6:3, 2:4 (ESV)

This is the One who gave everything to claim me as His very own. His love has won my heart. The Father asks, "will you have this Man?" And I simply reply, "Yes."

Looking for that blessed hope and glorious appearing of our great God and our Savior, Jesus Christ, who gave Himself to redeem us and to purify for Himself a people that are His very own.

Titus 2:13-14 (NKJV)

ဆ . ၛ

"Why did it take me so long to share this favorite spot with you?"

It was the same beach. The same cove. The same place I had walked and prayed and recognized the voice of the LORD to my heart.

There will be mountains to climb. But I will be with you.
Treasure what is right in front of you.
Trust Me with the trials.

But this time I wasn't alone. My husband was right beside me.

Leaning against a large boulder near the water's edge, he pulled me in close. I sunk into his full embrace. The breeze tossed my hair across his face, but he didn't move. The gentle lapping of the surf was so soothing. The little sandpipers flitting from rock to rock around us were fun to watch. But for us it was precious stillness. Peace. Rest.

It was his only chance to breathe in the middle of a hard-fought season. A wearying stretch of time, in every sense of the word, for both of us! In just a few days, he would close the door of his office of seven years for the last time, having put in long hours and late nights in these final days to finish well, with integrity and honor.

A new chapter was just around the corner. A new job opportunity. A fresh start. The long prayed-for chance to shift gears, to welcome a new challenge.

We exhaled, lingering in that embrace. We breathed in peace and whispered back gratefulness! "I want to remember this day," I said softly. He held me a little tighter and nodded.

Lyrics from our wedding processional twenty years prior spoke the praise of our hearts:

Praise to the Lord, the Almighty,
the King of creation!
O my soul, praise Him,
for He is thy health and salvation!
All ye who hear,
now to His temple draw near,
praise Him in glad adoration.

Praise to the Lord who o'er all
things so wondrously reigneth,
shelters thee under His wings,
yea, so gently sustaineth!
Hast thou not seen
how thy desires e'er have been
granted in what He ordaineth?

Praise to the Lord, who doth
prosper thy work and defend thee,
surely His goodness and mercy
here daily attend thee.
Ponder anew
what the Almighty can do,
if with His love He befriend thee.

Praise to the Lord,
O let all that is in me adore Him!
All that has life and breath,
come now with praises before Him.
Let the Amen
sound from His people again,
gladly for aye, we adore Him.

Joachim Neander, 1650–1680
Tr. by Catherine Winkworth, 1829–1878

೮೦ . ೦೪

As we turn the page into this new chapter, we acknowledge the LORD's faithful and gracious hand in and through it all. We praise Him. We thank Him. May all that is in us adore Him!

Leaning on our Rock, our precious LORD JESUS, *both of us* surrounded by His embrace—*held and beloved.*

೮೦ . ೦೪

Read more of their stories . . . and reflect on your own!

REBEKAH
Genesis 24

What gave Rebekah the courage to travel with a stranger to a foreign land, to become the wife of a man she had never met?

What free gifts had he offered her? What prompted her to receive them with joy rather than doubt?

What had she been told about Isaac and Abraham that touched her heart?

What was her reply?

What was her greatest longing as she made the long journey to meet Him?

THE BRIDE OF CHRIST
Ephesian 5:21–33, I Corinthians 13:1–13, I John 4:19 (CHRIST's love for the church), Revelation 19:6–9 (marriage supper of the Lamb)

What free gift does JESUS freely offer His bride?

What does He reveal about His heart in His tireless pursuit of hers?

What causes the Bride of CHRIST to treasure Him as precious, when she has yet to see Him face to face?

How is she getting to know Him and drawing ever closer to Him while she waits for that day?

OVERALL
Psalm 34:2–10, Song of Solomon 6:3, 2:4, Titus 2:13–14, 1 Peter 2:7

What have you learned about GOD the Father and His Son JESUS that touches your heart?

How have you seen the hand of GOD or felt His Spirit move, drawing your heart toward His?

What reassures you that His banner over you is love?

What Scriptures might steady your heart and remind you that when life feels impossible, He holds what is unholdable, and more importantly He holds you, tenderly cared for and secure in His embrace? That one day you will see Him face to face, that He will take you by the hand and lead you Home?

℘ . ℭ

Who is this One we are getting to know more intimately? The LORD revealed Himself to Rebekah and to those who call Him precious as:

* the One who goes before us to prepare the way
* the One who positions our hearts to receive His best
* the One who reveals enough of His heart to win ours
* the One who draws our hearts to simply say "yes!"
* the One whose face we long to see
* the One who fixes our eyes on the horizon
* the One who loves us like no other!

Chapter Ten

the One you love . . . blessed are you when you tell His story!

Pause for a moment and think of that special someone in *your* life.

Your face lights up when you say their name. Your heart skips a beat when they smile, especially in your direction. You hate goodbyes and eagerly anticipate every new hello. You can't wait to spend time with them. You devote hours listening to their stories, sharing your own, getting to know each other deeply.

You let them take you on the wildest adventures and invest in lessons to learn their favorite activity so you can enjoy it together. You fix things just the way they like them because you know it touches their heart. When you overflow with details about them or the times you've spent together, friends and family just tilt their head with a knowing smile and indulge you because they know this is your heart.

This is love.

It could be a spouse, or a child, or a parent, friend, or mentor. This person has impacted you in unique and special ways. You respect them. You enjoy them. You learn from them. There is a heart-to-heart connection, an unspoken understanding, and yet something fresh and new that helps you grow in unexpected ways.

They bring out the best in you. You trust them. They mean the world to you and nothing brings you greater joy than to know you mean the world to them too.

All of the above is true of your Savior too!

It is LOVE. His love for you. And your love for Him!

The response of your heart to the One who has become precious to you.

We love because He first loved us.

I John 4:19 (NIV, ESV)

What greater story do you have to tell?

Echoes. Through time. Across generations. Women, just like you, rejoice in telling their stories! (Men too!) Stories that are unique and intimate. Stories rooted in heartache and struggle where courageous faith is birthed. Stories that point to one place. To the One who transcends time and circumstance. The One who is weaving strands of the greatest love story ever told. It started with His Son and builds with every new heart that is drawn to trust Him. Drawn by cords of love, not force, and held with strength and power that is also tender and abundantly generous!

ℬ . ℭ

John chapter 9 tells the story of a man who was born blind. For decades he had only seen darkness. Until he met JESUS and miraculously received his sight!

Neighbors and acquaintances couldn't believe the transformation. They were so stunned that they tried to convince themselves this couldn't be the same person. But the man insisted,

"Yes! I am the same one who used to sit and beg! I was blind, but now I can see!"[41]

His story prompted a lot of questions. "Who healed you?" "How did this happen?"[42]

The man with new eyes had few answers. "I don't know,"[43] was all he could say. Over and over. But his limited knowledge didn't diminish the power of his story. He clearly and joyfully declared his own experience. Again and again.

I was blind, but now I can see!

John 9:25

The religious leaders hounded the man with more questions. They demanded that he tell what had happened to him. More than once. They debated about the One who could perform such healing. For they considered the LORD JESUS in breach of the law because He "worked" on the Sabbath. They counted Him as a common sinner, who couldn't possibly perform such a miracle.

Again, the man had few answers. But as he responded to each new wave of questions, his story became more real to him. His voice became stronger. Before long, this man who was blind and likely disregarded more than he was heard, was boldly proclaiming the truth and reality of GOD in the face of severe opposition from the leaders of the synagogue:

"Why do you want to hear my story again? Do you want to become His disciples too? He healed my eyes, and yet you do not know where He comes from? We know that GOD doesn't listen to sinners, but He is ready to hear those who worship Him and do His will. Ever since the world began, no one has been able to open the eyes of someone born blind. If this Man were not from GOD, He couldn't have done it!"[44]

The Jewish leaders, offended by this man's boldness and his spoken truth that condemned them, threw him out of the synagogue. JESUS didn't leave the man to sort through the events of that eventful day on his own. He pursued a second encounter with him. Face to face, JESUS asked him, "do you believe in Me?" The man replied, "Yes, LORD, I believe!"[45] And he worshiped JESUS.

Even when others refused to hear, this man told his story. With confidence that would not be deterred. No one could deny him the reality he had just lived! As he struggled to explain what happened to him, I believe GOD's Spirit gave him words. As he heard the truth about the One who healed him, spoken from his own lips, his faith increased and his voice became stronger and stronger!

The response of the Jewish leaders recorded in Scripture was only rejection and persecution. But I wonder if there were others standing by, watching what unfolded and hearing this man's testimony who were drawn to know and trust the Savior? It is entirely possible! The LORD JESUS Himself stated that this man's circumstances were purposely orchestrated by the Father so that "the power of GOD could be seen in him!"[46]

This dear man encountered the LORD JESUS and he was never the same again. Nothing would take away the healing he received. The power of his own story deepened his understanding of the reality of GOD in his life, the impossible healing he received in his physical body, and the transformation that took place in his heart!

ॐ . ॐ

Have these *Held and Beloved* stories impacted your heart? Helped you recognize the miraculous parts of your own story? Encouraged you to notice the hand of GOD moving and working in your life? Sharpened your vision to trace His handiwork and His eternal purposes that are always moving forward? Have these stories won your heart to value the beauties of the One who loves you more than any other, knowing you hold a unique and precious place in His plan?

Let these stories ignite a passion in you to *tell your own story* of being *Held and Beloved* by Him!

How has the LORD JESUS made Himself real to you? Done the impossible in your physical body? Met you in a dark place and declared you free of condemnation? Reassured you that no brokenness in your story deters His plan for you or disqualifies you from being chosen for that special part only you can play in His purposes?

How has GOD provided for you in ways that display His limitlessness? Shown you that in His plan, there is no dead end, and it is never too late?

When has the LORD knowingly called you into a storm? How did He meet you in the middle of the raging seas? What surprisingly precious discoveries about His heart did you make on that frightening journey? How did His strength or His truth empower you to step out with courage?

Has there been a time when you felt He simply came close to hold you and let you grieve? To weep with you? How did your heart respond to His comfort? To what fresh path did He point as you bravely stepped forward from that place of sorrow?

How have you heard the LORD's voice, clearly and unmistakably speaking to your heart? What impact has one-on-one dialogue with the Savior had on your healing, growth, or vision of the future?

What has the LORD called you to surrender? How has He won your trust, your heart? What has drawn you to join others who declare that He is precious?

What story has He given you to tell, in your own way? To bear witness of the reality of GOD in *your* life? Why not pause (right now!) to ask the LORD how you can share your experience?

It may be as simple as a one-on-one conversation with a friend, a family member, a neighbor, or even a stranger in the grocery store. Maybe it's time for you to be vulnerable and open up in a small group? Or speak your testimony to a larger gathering? Maybe you will find new courage to share your experience through social media, to put the highlight reel on hold to get real and share the deeper parts of your heart? Or allow your love for the LORD to inspire something creative that expresses what means most to you? Trust that the One who created you and won your heart will be faithful to show you how to tell your own story about JESUS. To give others a glimpse of His glory!

∞ . ∞

Stories are powerful. Captivating. Relatable. Comforting. Enlightening. Challenging. Personal. Warm and inviting.

The most interesting stories tell of wondrous transformation. Rescue. Healing. HOPE.

The best stories tell of the GOD who created us, who knows us intimately, who gave His own Son to be our Savior. The Almighty One who values every one of us. The One whose love stops at nothing to pursue our hearts. The One whose power and faithfulness win our enduring trust. The One who moves and works in our lives in wondrous ways. Priceless ways. Granting us glimpses of glory and gifts of joy with which nothing can compare!

If this is true for you, then you don't want anyone else to miss the opportunity to experience the same redeeming power and boundless love in their own life! Your story is powerful! Your personal testimony can help someone else find their own path to the Savior! For the believers who are listening, your story can help them better understand their own. To find the courage to share their own struggles and victories. To treasure their relationship with GOD and hunger to know Him better.

Join the chorus of praise to our GOD. Tell of His mighty works as displayed in *your* life. Finding words for your experiences will bring you more JOY than you can imagine! Especially when the cry of your heart meets the deep need of another.

Each time you bear witness to the reality of GOD, you honor Him. Each time you encourage another to place their trust in Him, you touch His heart. You mean the world to Him and nothing brings Him greater joy than to hear you say that He means the world to you too!

Your face lights up when you speak His name. You let Him take you on the wildest adventures. You work hard to do things just the way He asks because you know it brings delight to His heart. He has impacted you in unique and special ways. There is a heart-to-heart connection, an unspoken understanding, yet always something fresh and new that helps you grow in unexpected ways.

He brings out the best in you. You trust Him. You declare that He is precious!

Don't keep the Love of your life a secret.

Find your voice. Tell your story!

Praise the Lord for His loving kindness, and for His wonderful works to the children of men!
Psalm 107:31 (ESV)

Go and tell what great things the Lord has done for you!

Luke 8:39 (ESV)

Afterthoughts

O our God, we thank You and praise Your glorious Name! But who am I, that I should give anything to You? Everything we have has come from You, and we can give You only what You have already given us!

I Chronicles 29:13-14

What a precious, precious thought! What I bring to offer the LORD is exactly what He has placed in my hands to give. So, I should not be shy in bringing it.

That posture is so uncharacteristic of me. I am painfully shy. Always second-guessing. Driven to perfection. Wanting so desperately to get it right! Especially anything I offer to the LORD. For, to me, He is precious and He is worthy of the absolute best I could ever present to Him.

Simple as it may seem, I can thank a True Value Hardware commercial for a revolutionary shift in my thinking! A mom and her young son are shopping for a Christmas gift. The boy is diligent, insisting to the salesman that they *must* find the one thing his dad will really, really, *really* love! The flash forward to

Christmas morning shows the dad opening his gift, looking over the boy's head, catching his mom's eye with a knowing glance, then meeting the boy's expectant gaze with the biggest smile, saying, "Wow! I really, really, *really* love this! Thank you!" The dad engulfs his son, who collapses into his father's arms with a look of deep pride and glee!

The scene helps me picture something completely different than my fretful hesitancy. I can now see myself as a beloved child of GOD. Not shy at all. But like an innocent child, who has tucked away in some secret place to slave over creating something they are convinced their loved one will really, really, *really* love! Who cannot contain themselves to wait another second to thrust it into their hands, beaming with anticipation of their overjoyed response!

I want to create with that depth of love for my LORD. That abundant confidence. Not in me. But in the unique person GOD has created me to be and the gifts He places in my hands to offer back to Him!

Just a few months ago, these thoughts emboldened my heart as the annual Christmas program at our church approached. My husband and I were on the program to sing. The day before, racked with nerves, I started to pray.

"Dear LORD, you know my heart. My greatest desire for this program is that it will tell Your story the way You want it to be told. That it will touch the hearts of any who are in attendance and draw them to You. But can I come to You now, just as Your child. You have given me a love of singing. I so long to feel Your power flowing through me, filling me with all the fullness of GOD, settling these nerves, freeing me to sing with JOY to You!"

Getting ready at home the morning of the program, I paused by the little Christmas tree in our bedroom window. Lost in the soft glow of the tree lights, and the music and lyrics of Selah's

"Wonderful Merciful Savior," my whole being simply adored Him. I sang along with JOY and a full voice! I prayed again that I could sing from that same genuine place in my heart during the program.

My heart raced as our place in the program neared. I prayed again, bold enough for the first time to ask for such a blessing just for me, as His child. A wave of peace washed over me as we stood to sing. I glanced upward and found myself lost in the twinkle lights that lined the ceiling, feeling His love just for me! I truly sang with freedom and JOY bursting from my insides, every part of me overwhelmed by the goodness of GOD, the gift of our Savior!

> *O how I love Him,*
> *how I adore Him!*
> *my breath, my sunshine,*
> *my All in All!*
> *the Great Creator*
> *became my Savior,*
> *and all God's fullness*
> *dwelleth in Him!*

"Down from His Glory" —
William E. Booth-Clibborn, 1921

Friends said they had never seen my face beam with such joy. I floated on a cloud of utter gratefulness for my Savior for the rest of that day! I felt sure He was whispering to me, *"I really, really, really loved it!"*

Newfound confidence. Knowing I delight His heart. It is powerful. And inspiring!

I welcomed January wondering if this could be the year that I write with more confidence just like I felt new freedom to sing? With confidence that is not in me, but in Him, a pouring out that cannot keep silent, coming from a place that is held and beloved by Him?

There is great joy in telling my story! I am so thankful for the opportunity to testify of the reality of GOD in my life. To bear witness of His wondrous love and powerful redemption.

This book is my not-so-shy offering to Him. I pray it delights His heart!

A word of thanks . . .

To my one and only Editor, the Writer of my story! My favorite moments are tucked away with the LORD JESUS. I can't fully describe the beauty of time spent "in a bubble" with Him, sitting at my dining room table turned writing desk, trusting Him to guide these words. I pray that telling my story touches His heart, that it brings Him the honor and glory due His Name!

To my husband, David, my daughter, Emily, and my son, Ben, who share my earthly journey toward our heavenly Home. Even more than "my" story, the one all four of us are living lights up my insides. They were the ones who gave me the courage to start a blog four years ago, to tell my story of JESUS, one precious lesson at a time!

To Dad & Mom Stewart and Mom Colaiuta. I cherish the thought that the three of them were the first to lay eyes on these words, from the very first draft. Their encouragement and watchful eye for authenticity and accuracy to Scripture are invaluable. Their love and prayers are priceless gifts! To Dad Colaiuta, at Home in heaven ahead of us, who sweetly told me one day that although few of his earnest prayers had been answered over his lifetime, I had been one of them.

To my brother, Dave, and my sisters, Sue, Mandy, Roe, Jen, & Jan, and Beth, Gwen & Mona. I am so grateful for the many times they have fielded my texts, faithfully prayed for me, cried with me, rejoiced with me, and lifted my heart to the Father! (For the record, my brothers-in-law, nephews and nieces all mean the world to me too!)

To my favorite coffee date, Renate, whose wisdom of years and love of a good story (usually real and raw or hilariously funny!) captivate every Tuesday or Thursday we are blessed to linger at my kitchen table!

To my Ardsley Sunday school girls who first captured my heart and instilled in me the longing to speak GOD's truth into the lives of other women, to surround them with compassion, the extra mile to meet practical needs, and love that overflows!

To my sweet summer study group friends who gathered in my living room to dig deep into the stories of these women in the Bible. I am still moved by poignant moments from our conversations, their brave vulnerability and hunger to know GOD's heart. I will always treasure the sisterhood I was given to hold right here in my own home for those months.

To the "ground angels" the LORD has sent to surround me at every turn, over many years. They have been the hands, feet and heart of JESUS, loved on me, spoken life and truth over me, prayed for me, and pointed me faithfully to the One who gives me every reason to hope! Each of them holds a sweet spot in my story! . . .

. . . dear friends in Philly from second grade to high school, extended family at Bryn Mawr & Hatboro, my University of Delaware roommate and Intervarsity leaders, co-workers at Merck, Tuesday and Friday night Bible study groups in Ardsley, and youth conference friends at Brandywine Chapel and Greenwood Hills,

. . . in Williamsport, playgroup moms, kind neighbors and church friends I still hold dear,

. . . in Savannah, our church family at Faith Bible Chapel, fellow homeroom moms and dance friends, and precious ladies who welcomed me into their study group at Independent Presbyterian Church,

. . . last but certainly not least, a growing circle of dear friends and neighbors in south Florida, including our church

family at Grace & Truth, and fellow class members and leaders in Bible Study Fellowship, who have become some of my closest confidantes.

To new friends in the writing world, Amy & Sara, Erin, Christie & Lisa-Jo, and Malinda. Their passion for speaking GOD's truth through words inspires me to keep my knees on the floor, my nose in the Book, and my computer standing by to collect and share discoveries as He unfolds new chapters of my story.

To the team at WestBow Press, beginning with my very first conversation with a kind gentleman named Stephan, and his sweet wife, Josie, who have faithfully prayed for this project. Their eternal perspective and confidence in the Father's plan keep my eyes fixed on the LORD JESUS, with the determination to work hard, stay humble, and watch where He will send this story!

I thank my God upon every remembrance of you, always in every prayer of mine for you, making request with joy, for your partnership in the gospel from the first day until now. Being confident of this very thing: that He who began a good work in you will be faithful to complete it . . . it is right for me to think this of you, because I have you in my heart.

Philippians 1:3–7 (NKJV)

Endnotes

1   James 2:23
2   Genesis 17:15
3   Genesis 18:15
4   Genesis 18:14
5   Luke 1:25
6   John 8:7
7   John 8:10–11
8   John 8:11
9   Hebrews 12:1
10 Romans 6:1 (KJV)
11 Joshua 2:9, 11–13 (ESV)
12 John 4:16
13 John 4:20, 25 (ESV)
14 John 4:29 (ESV)
15 Mark 5:28
16 Mark 5:30
17 Mark 5:34
18 2 Kings 4:28
19 Esther 2:10 (NLT, paraphrase)
20 Luke 1:38
21 Ruth 1:20
22 Ruth 3:9
23 Ruth 3:18
24 John 11:22
25 John 11:34
26 John 11:41–45 (ESV)
27 Genesis 16:8
28 Genesis 16:8

29 Genesis 16:13 (ESV)
30 Genesis 21:17–18 (ESV)
31 John 13:7 (NLT, paraphrase)
32 Job 13:15 (NKJV)
33 John 20:13
34 John 20:15
35 John 20:16
36 John 20:17
37 I Samuel 1:17 (ESV)
38 John 12:3
39 Genesis 24:50–51
40 Genesis 24:58
41 John 9:9, 11
42 John 9:10
43 John 9:12
44 John 9:27, 30–33
45 John 9:35–38
46 John 9:3